REAL LIFE:REAL SPICE

REAL LIFE : REAL SPICE
THE OFFICIAL STORY
BY THE SPICE GIRLS

THANKS TO

Jackie Adams
Louise Adams
Christian Adams
Pauline Bunton
Paul Bunton
Andi Brown
Danielle Brown
Catri Drummond
Dazed and Confused
James Freedman
Noam Friedlander
Simon Fuller
Natalie Halliwell
Camilla Howarth
Sally Hudson
Dorian Lynskey
Joan O'Neill
Paul O'Neill
Rachel Pinfold
Emma Poole
Gerrard Tyrrell

PHOTOGRAPHY

The Spice Girls' families
Alex Bailey
Richard Bloomfield
Ray Burmiston
Michael Ginsberg
Tim Hetherington
Simon Jacobs
Peter Langford
Martin Norris
Pictorial Press
Terry Richards
Jeff Roberts
Frank Spooner Pictures
Rankin Waddell

DESIGN

Tim Barnes
Katherine Tulloh

WORDS

The Spice Girls
Rebecca Cripps
Mal Peachey @ JMP

SPICE GIRLS MANAGEMENT

Simon Fuller @ 19 Management

First published in 1997 by
Zone/Chameleon Books
an imprint of Andre Deutsch Ltd.
a member of tthe VCI plc Group
106 Great Russell Street
London WCIB 3LJ
in association with **19 Management Ltd**

CIP Data for this title is available from the British Library

ISBN 0223 99299 5

19

MANAGEMENT LIMITED

Hey Spice Squad!

Are you ready for another Spice Book? Then read on!

Real Life:Real Spice is where you'll find out all about our lives when we were growing up - what made us tick as kids, our early ambitions and how we made it to where we are now. And, for the first time ever, our brothers and sisters speak frankly about what it was like to live with us when we were wannabes.

This book is full of exclusive stuff about what we're really like, where we're coming from, and where we're headed. **Real Life:Real Spice** is a must for all SuperSpicers, so thanks for buying it and we hope you have as much of a giggle reading it as we did putting it together... Enjoy!

love Geri x

love Melanie xCx

Big kisses Emma xxx

Mel B

love Victoria x.

19 MANAGEMENT LIMITED, RANELAGH DOCK... GRANGE... LONDON SW10 4NP   Telephone 0171 384 1882   Facsimile 0171 376 2602
Registered Office: Hanover House 14 Hanover Square London W1   Registered No. 1902942
Vat No: 61 432 7269 14

"This book is dedicated to our families, friends and, of course, our fans."

In the Beginning

ONCE UPON A TIME there were no Spice Girls. Just five little girls, each very different, but each with their own special talents and dreams and a touch of star quality...

Emma

EARLIEST MEMORIES

"My earliest memory is of being in a pushchair when I was a baby. It was raining heavily and I had a plastic sheet over me. I remember feeling really warm inside and watching the rain splash against the plastic while my poor mum was pushing me along. She was completely soaked."

"I can't tell you how much I enjoyed modelling. I used to take my friends with me and let them have a go – they used to love it. In these ones I was probably laughing at my mum."

"Baring all for Mothercare. I was such a poseur!"

"The Disco Queen and Steve Davis! Sometimes when I was modelling, my brother PJ got in on the act when he saw how much fun I was having."

MY LITTLE BROTHER, PJ

"He was so good as a child. When he was about two we'd all be watching telly and suddenly we'd notice he'd disappeared, then find him walking to bed with his blanket and bottle all on his own. He was bad sometimes, though. I had my room specially painted once, with flowers, a tree and a bunny rabbit on the wall. I loved it because it was like being in a garden, which we never had. But just after it was done, my brother and our little cousin came in and drew all over it in lipstick. I was gutted because it stained all the walls and we never got it off. A few years later, I came back from a modelling job to find that my dad had redecorated my whole bedroom with pink clouds. I loved it. I even had the duvet to match.

"I remember PJ hitting me with a tambourine once. I just hit him back with it. It was a strange weapon, but it made a great sound! We argued quite a lot when we were younger, but we get on really well now. It's lovely. We can rely on each other. I'm always asking him to parties with me and I get on really well with his girlfriend. He always got on well with my boyfriends, too. Sometimes I'd be sitting in my room and my brother and boyfriend would be in his room chatting and playing computer games. I'd shout: 'Excuse me! Hello! I exist!' Still, it was quite nice sometimes, because it meant I could chill out with my mum or have a bath."

First Day at School

"On my first day of school, with my pigtails. I thought it was just another dressing up game until I got there and realised it was school... Oh no!"

FIRST FRIENDS

"My best friends at primary school were Fiona and Sara. I did modelling from quite an early age and one girl hated me for it. She used to bring in the catalogue and say: 'Look at Emma. She's just showing off. She thinks she's great.' I got really upset about that, even though I lived for modelling. I'd go to my mum and sob: 'Mum, I'm not showing off. I like doing it.' Still, Fiona always stuck up for me and said to the girl: 'I bet you wish you were doing it. That's why you're so mean.' She was cool.

"Sports days were very important when we were really young. You had to win. But I always came second because Fiona was so fantastic at sports. She'd shout, 'Come on Emma, come on,' during the race, but I never beat her, even in swimming.

"There was a big gang of us where I lived and we'd go out and play all the time. We'd meet in the den we set up on the grass, or down at the brook. We had a rope swing over the brook, which was excellent fun, even though I fell in a few times. I had a brilliant childhood."

RIGHT: FROM TOP
"The day I was baptised. I had flowers to hold and lots of presents from my family."

~

"This was my second birthday with all my friends at our little tea party – wicked!"

~

"With all my friends on my sixth birthday. I was so lucky to have so many friends, and I always loved having parties and people staying over... so I always got lots of presents!"

NAUGHTY GIRLS

"I was really naughty during a lunch break once. We had tap-dancing in the same classroom as we had art and everyone's pictures were up on the walls. My friend Aaron and I sprayed the whole room with a fire extinguisher. After school we had a special assembly where we were told that nobody was allowed to leave the building until the teachers found out who'd done it. It was a very strict school and if they'd found us out, we would have been expelled, so we didn't own up. We should have, though."

FAVE GAMES

"We played England, Ireland, Scotland, Wales with elastic, hopskotch and skipping games. In skipping, I remember chanting: 'Tea and coffee, coffee and tea, I want Fiona (my best friend) in with me.' Everyone used to be waiting around to get in, but we'd never let them. We also played chase where the boys lifted up the girls' skirts – I always made sure I was wearing nice knickers for that. I wasn't that good at football and I became known for kicking the boys if they didn't let me play. Not long ago I saw one of the boys from school and he just said: 'Stay away!' It hit me then, that I used to kick them properly where it hurt and shout: 'I wanna play football!' I loved rounders and Fiona and I were quite good at netball, too."

DON'T FEEL WELL

"I had really bad chickenpox. I was covered from head to toe in spots – it was so bad I couldn't move. My mum had to carry me out to the back of the car on the way to the doctor. I remember her saying: 'If you scratch them, you're going to be scarred.' I tried not to, but I did end up with some scars."

LEFT
"My brother and I on holiday in Corsica."
BELOW
"I always had lots of presents at Christmas – this was my first makeup kit. I sat my brother down and dressed him up. I think he liked it at the time but I don't know if he would let me do it now!"

CHRISTMAS

"I always got loads of presents at Christmas because I've got quite a big family. I'd have a big pillowcase full of them. Once I'd opened them, I'd jump on my mum and dad shouting, "Look what I got!" and show them everything, not realising they'd probably been up an hour before, wrapping it all up. I got a walking, talking doll and a Barbie house with a lift, which I loved. I believed in Father Christmas for quite a while and I could never sleep on Christmas Eve because I was looking out for him. One night I was convinced I saw him flying through the sky."

MY BIG SISTER, EMMA
by PJ Bunton

"My first proper memory of Emma was when she was at stage school and I was about five or six. When I went up there, I saw her during breaks. She was always really nice to me and so were all her friends. They used to pick me up, kiss and cuddle me and say: 'Isn't he cute?'

"I liked acting and performing, but not as much as Emma did. She was always much more into it. When I went with my mum to pick her up from school, she'd have her mates in the back of the car and they'd act out little plays for us. They were always very funny.

"We used to have arguments, but most of the time she was a very loving sister. We'd argue about silly things: cake missing from the fridge, who was going to sleep on the top bunk, who was going to sit in the front of the car. We never really fought physically – just a little slap on the arm, nothing serious.

"If we ever had an argument and then heard our mum walk in, we'd run into our bedroom, wipe the tears away and then be all lovey-dovey again. We didn't like to get mum involved because if she stuck up for one of us, then the other one would get the hump and there would be another argument. We never wanted that to happen.

"We shared a room for quite a while, 'til Emma was about 12 or 13. I had to go to bed before her, because I was younger, so I was always asleep when she came in. Sometimes we had arguments when we were getting up about whether to wait for a lift to school and risk being late and then get told off. I didn't really mind if I was late or not, but Emma did. I think she worked quite hard at school. She worked harder than me, anyway – I preferred the practical lessons.

"Emma's always stuck up for me. If she ever overheard me having an argument with a friend, she'd come in and break it up. She helps a lot. She's always been my 'big' sister, the one who would help me out if I needed her. I'd never need to ask anybody else."

"One Christmas she was given a little doll's dressing table and the first thing she did was sit me down and dress me up. She put a little hat and coat on me and make-up all over my face. I don't remember it too well, but I know I never let her do it again.

"She's very generous and always buys me good presents – she's given me watches and tracksuits and trainers. We always used to have a laugh when we got terrible pyjamas and gloves from our grannies."

LITTLE REBEL

"I used to try and hitch my skirt up at school, but I wasn't allowed to so I'd have to lower it after a while. Three days a week we'd wear a grey skirt, a white shirt and a red jumper and two days we'd have tracksuits, which was wicked. I loved waving goodbye to my brother in his school uniform when I was wearing my tracksuit."

"Sylvia Young – the best school ever. Most of my best friends came from here and I learnt so much – a wicked six years."

Sylvia Young Theatre School

SCHOOL DAYS

"I hated maths and history. Dance was always my favourite subject. We had a brilliant dance teacher called David Samuel. Everyone fancied him and couldn't wait for his class. Kelly Bright and I were good friends at school. We often bunked the other classes and when the headmistress came along David would hide us and say: 'No I haven't seen them today.' Even after school, everyone would go along to his classroom and stay for hours. He held dance auditions that went on for ages. If he put his hand on your shoulder you were out. Once Kelly and I danced from the beginning of the day right up to the end of the day and we actually felt sick because we'd been dancing so hard. We won, though. We were well proud.

"Sylvia Young was quite a small school and everyone knew each other. A lot of people think that stage schools must be really competitive, but it wasn't like that at all. If you had an audition, everyone would come up and wish you good luck for it. Even on my first day someone came up and said: 'Hi, how are you?' There was quite a bit of air kissing and all that, but everyone was really nice. My class was like a team and none of us ever seemed to argue. Still, there were a lot of kids who didn't really want to be there, but their mums wanted them to be little Shirley Temples. You could tell the kids who wanted to do it from the kids who didn't want to, even though we all still had a laugh because it was such good fun.

"My mum couldn't afford Sylvia's school for a little while and I had to go to a normal one. The shock to my system was scary. I cried so much. The divisions in the class were awful – the nerds in one corner, the cool people in another and the hippies in another. Sylvia's was never like that. I was only there for a week, though. I had a friend called Alan who phoned the headmistress and said that he'd spoken to me and I was really upset and not happy at school. So she let me back in the school. I feel as though all the people from that school will always be there for me."

AMBITION

"I was a real poser from the age of three and always wanted to be a dancer."

"More of my modelling things, which I loved. I had so much fun shouting and smiling and I always had a McDonalds after."

EXAMS

"If we had an audition, there would be some of us who'd wash our hair in the sink and make sure we looked really nice, and others who'd go home and tell their mums that they got lost and couldn't make it. Sometimes I'd phone my mum and tell her I was really tired that day. She'd always say: 'Okay. If you don't feel like doing it, come home.' She never pushed me. I went to dancing classes from a really early age and she'd sometimes try and stop me going because she was worried I'd get tired. But I'd say: 'No! I've got to go. I really want to!' Of course, if she'd said that I had to go, I wouldn't have! If you tell someone to do something, they'll always do the opposite.

"I didn't really get scared before exams. I did revise, but I found it so boring. I remember during my GCSEs, I walked into school late because I'd been having breakfast with my friend Kelly down the road. I strolled in and suddenly realised that we had an art exam that day. I really was quite bad. I didn't fail anything, though, and I did well in drama, dance and singing. You know when you know you want to do something, and if you're going to fail in that, you don't want to do anything else. That's what I was like. It wasn't that I didn't bother with anything else. I liked English and art and maths sometimes, even though I wasn't very good at them. I was always willing to learn in things like French, but I never got anywhere."

POP STARS

"I loved Matt Goss from Bros, and thought Kevin Rowlands, the lead singer of Dexy's Midnight Runners was well cool."

TELLY

"I always had to be home to watch *Neighbours*. I liked *Grange Hill* because a few of my friends were in it. I loved *Blind Date* and couldn't miss it. I still like it."

FOOD

"We had nice food at school. There was a small canteen that served jacket potatoes and sandwiches, but mostly I just used to eat chipsticks. We played donut games where you had to eat a whole donut without licking your lips. The one thing we weren't allowed was chewing gum."

PJ: *"I can't remember if she always had such a sweet tooth. She loved Pepsi and used to drink gallons of it at a time. We both loved Chinese food. Whenever Mum asked us what we wanted for dinner, we used to shout: 'Chinese!' We'd get it quite often as well, because my dad liked it, too."*

"My gorgeous brother PJ and I at Finchley Fair. I thought I was so cool in my off-the-shoulder dress."

BOYFRIENDS

"I had a big crush on a boy called Cole, who later had a part on *Eastenders*. I fancied him forever and ever. He was lovely – very sweet and boyish. Then, one day when we'd just left school, he asked me out. But it was too late because I was with somebody else by then. Why does that always happen? Generally, though, I've been lucky with boys. It usually takes me ages to get the person I want and then I get them and they fall in love with me and I wonder if I want them anymore!"

PJ: *"When I first started seeing girls, I sometimes asked Emma's advice about what to do. She'd ask what the girl was like and what she did and then she'd give her opinion. It always got me there! She was always really nice to my girlfriends. The first boyfriend of hers I remember meeting was Nick. He was good bloke, although he could be a bit loud sometimes. He used to come into my room and chat and play on the computer. In fact, I've always got on well with Emma's boyfriends."*

TEENAGER

PJ: *"She only changed a little bit when she became a teenager. She went out more often. We never spoke much back then because she was always out and when she came in, I'd go out. She got into clothes, especially Naf Naf, Chevignon and all those old labels. Years ago one Christmas I bought her what I thought was a Naf Naf tracksuit, but it turned out just to be a Naff tracksuit from the market. She was a little bit upset about that!*

"We didn't go out together much, but we would go to the school discos. Emma used to love them because she likes to dance and have a good time with her mates. But really we just did our own things."

MODELLING

"Modelling trips were really fun. There would be loads of kids and we had parties all the time. The last night, there would always be a fancy dress party, and the whole time we were there we'd be getting ready for that. We went away for two weeks but we'd only work every other day, so we had loads of time off to chill, make songs up, form bands and mess around."

DAYS OUT

"At weekends I often went rollerskating with Kelly at Ally Pally, which was just up the road. We used to go on rowing boats there, too, and visit the farm.

"On Kelly's birthday once we went to the Video Café in Central London. It was quite a posh café with screens all round the walls playing pop videos. I thought it was brilliant because I'd never been anywhere like that before. Another time she had a sleepover. It was wicked."

WORKING

"I had a weekend job for a couple of years helping a rich old lady out. My mum worked for her and went in every day and I'd go in on a Saturday and Sunday. I'd wash up for her and hoover and clean her silver. She'd never check it – I think she just liked the company. Sometimes I'd just go in and read her the paper. She was a bit moany, but she was nice, really. I was about 16 at the time and spent my wages on clothes."

"I spent all my holidays at Highfield caravan park in Clacton. Here I am with a friend having a wicked time."

Mel B

ALBUM: CLOCKWISE FROM TOP LEFT

~

"What a laugh! Here's me in one of my favourite dresses at a photo shoot. Check out the smile."

~

"Another photo shoot, and I'm holding on in case I fall off... aaahh!"

~

"This is me with my best Christmas present, when I was about four and a half – a nurse's oufit which I thought looked wicked. I also had some equipment in a nurse's first aid box to look after my new Tiny Tears doll."

~

"This is me and my sister Danielle. We'd had some sort of argument, so our smiles look really false!"

~

"This is me at my Aunty Pamela's in York, being very well behaved for a change."

~

"Slammin' reggae was my fave even at six. Check out the teeth!"

MY LITTLE SISTER, DANIELLE

"There's a five year age gap between my sister and me so she really was my 'little sister'. I always beat her up and tortured her – I was horrible to her. Once she tried to sneak in while I was in the bath, so I slammed the door on her and shut her fingers in it. I didn't care. I just thought it served her right for spying on me. The next day we had school photographs taken and my mum's still got the pictures of Danielle with her sore red hands placed in front of her. We're really, really alike, which is probably why we didn't get on as kids."

EARLIEST MEMORIES

"I remember that, for years and years from the age of about five, I dressed up in my mum's big sunglasses and wore a red cardigan over my head so that I could flick the arms like hair. I'd put a little red cardigan around my dog's head too and he'd play out with me. I've always loved clothes. When I was about six or seven my favourite shop was Tammy Girl. My mum worked in C&A, so she used to bring stuff home all the time.

"When I was about six, my dad told me that if I collected apple and orange pips I could make a tree grow five years later. So I saved up loads of pips for a couple of weeks and planted them in the garden."

ABOVE
"Me holding my brand new baby sister, Danielle. I love her!"
RIGHT
"Hey, look at me in a towelling nappy, thinking I'm the bee's knees!"

MY BIG SISTER, MEL
by Danielle Brown

"My first memory of Mel is from when I was about nine. Mum had said that she could paint her room and do loads of drawings on the walls, so while mum was out, Mel and her friend made me put my feet in black gloss paint. Then they lifted me up and made me walk on the ceiling, to leave footprints. I didn't want to do it at all. I had black paint on my feet for days afterwards.

"Melanie was always naughty and used to hit me. She would tease me about stupid little sister things. When I was in a mood, I didn't like anyone to touch me, so she used to prod me all the time and wind me up. Stuff like that.

"We never went to the same school at the same time. I think it was probably better that we didn't, because she would have embarrassed me in front of my friends and everybody. She used to say loads of stupid stuff in front of my friends. If I was embarrassed about having a boyfriend, she'd say: 'You've got a boyfriend!' I couldn't really get back at her because she always had something better to say.

"We used to go swimming a lot and she'd duck me under the water. I nearly drowned. She'd take me to the slide and push me really hard so I went flying. She'd think it was really funny, but I was really scared. I always got her back, even if it was ages later, by getting her in trouble with my dad. Then I knew she'd be grounded. If she did anything, I'd always say: 'You're gonna get done!' and that meant I'd tell my dad."

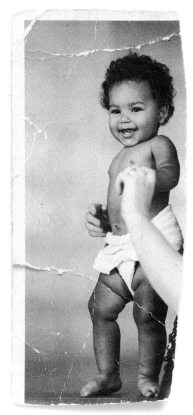

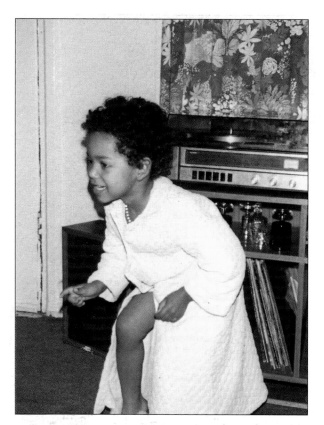

FIRST FRIENDS

"Sherelle was always a good friend. Her mum and my mum were best friends, so we practically grew up together. Rebecca was always one of my best friends and I still see her now. Charlotte, too.

"Sherelle and I used to nick Crunchies and penny sweets from the shop around the corner until one day we got caught, which was awful. I also went through a stage of not paying for my school dinners and keeping the money. Bad!

"Then Rebecca, and I fell out and didn't talk to each other for about seven months, which was very upsetting. I can't even remember what it was about - something really stupid. She used to send messages saying, 'Please be my friend' and I'd send a message back saying, 'No'. Then I'd think, 'Oh no', so I'd send a message back saying, 'I'm sorry, please be my friend now'. And she'd send a message back saying, 'No, not now. Too late'. It was pathetic. Then one day, we just made it up."

"This is what I used to do all the time – make up dances and show anyone and everyone who would watch."

"Look at the coconuts on that, then! Showing off my talents at an early age."

BORN TO DANCE

"I was seen at school as being a bit of a snob, because I was a dancer. Only thirty people in each year did dance, drama and music, so there were big divisions. People would call me 'Pineapple Head' at school because I wore my hair in a bun. They called me 'Bones' as well, because I was so thin. It never bothered me. I'd just shout back swear words."

NAUGHTY GIRLS

"Two doors down from our house was the Conservative Club, which didn't let black people in because it was so racist. It's still the same now. My mum and Berni dressed Sherelle and me up in tights and all-black outfits and we'd wait till 9.30pm when everyone passed our gates on the way to the club. Then we'd shout: 'Put 'em up!' and all these old bags would jump with shock. Once we went to the shop around the corner with plastic guns and pretended it was a hold-up. We were only about 12, but they believed us, so we had to take our masks off and say: 'It's only us!'

"I was once suspended for sending a nasty letter round the classroom about a girl. Isn't that horrible?"

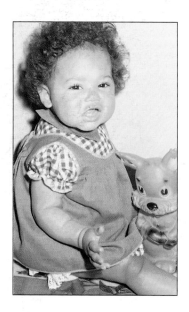

"Yes, I'm singing. I was always singing when I was a baby. My plastic dog used to really enjoy it."

POP STARS

"I was a big Neneh Cherry fan and wore four-colour rugby shirts and a medallion. My friend Rebecca, who is still my best friend today, was a Bros fan. I hated Bros, but I did get a leather jacket with zips on it because Rebecca said I had to."

"This is me on my sixth birthday. My mum made me a chocolate cake which I'm not too keen on, so I'm forcing a smile."

BIRTHDAY TREATS

"I went to other people's birthday parties when we were at junior school, but at senior school I never went because I heard they all snogged at parties. I found the idea disgusting and pathetic. Rebecca and I went to Pizzaland for my 14th or 15th birthday and had spritzers, then went to the cinema. Another birthday I had a sleepover and covered the floor of my room with mattresses, so it was like one big bed. It was excellent – a right laugh."

GAMES

"I was really good at Double Dutch when I was at school. We played Kiss-Catch but no-one ever ran after me. I thought it was revolting anyway. When anyone told me they'd kissed their boyfriend, I'd say: 'Yeugh! How can you do that?'"

"Me in a photo shoot looking and acting like a lady for a change."

TELEVISION

"I would never miss *Top of the Pops* or *Wildlife On One*, or if I did my dad would tape them for me. Finding out about how animals live and the process of their lives always fascinated me. I liked hospital programmes, too, when they showed actual surgery."

FOOD

"I used to like Wham Bars and Refreshers. I often had fish and chips in my dinner break because it was only 50p."

KIDS STUFF

"My mate Sherelle would come over and we'd record our own radio programmes in different foreign accents, or do little shows. Our mums were a right laugh. They'd dress up for us and we'd all have a fancy dress drama night together. Once I invited two friends round and my mum pretended to be a neurotic housewife and Sherelle pretended to be an Indian, with her hair up in a bun. Her mum, Berni, who was wearing my national Caribbean bright yellow and red costume with beads and a turban, sat there watching TV like a mad woman and I pretended to be normal. We kept it up all night. My friends just sat there for ages, then left the house thinking we were complete nutters. There was always madness in the house when Berni and Sherelle came round.

"I also made my first boyfriend dress up in my mum's clothes, with high heels and a necklace, and we watched all the cars stopping as he walked over to the shop. We did so many stupid things! We never spoke to our neighbours because they thought we were completely mad."

RIGHT: TOP TO BOTTOM

"I made Danielle dip her feet in paint then walk on the ceiling while I held her upside down. And she did it, bless her!"

~

"Mick Jagger lips on my bedroom wall done for me by my mate Regi, who is a wicked artist and designer."

~

"This sexy, stretchy lady is another one of Regi's paintings in my bedroom."

HOME

"Danielle and I shared a room for years. When it became officially mine, I had the walls painted with a pair of Mick Jagger lips, a rasta and a woman wearing a big feather boa. My friend Charlotte drew a really cool pair of Kicker boots, too. One day my mum tried to get creative and said, 'Look at this Melanie,' as she dipped her hand in some paint and ran her fingers up the wall. I said: 'Mum, that is pathetic.'

"One day my mum was artexing the walls when my dad came in from work. She said, 'Watch this!' and she dipped a paintbrush in white paint and splashed it all down my dad, who did not find it funny. My mum was rolling around in absolute hysterics, because she'd painted his hair and everything!"

"My lovely sister Danielle in my room that was covered all over with artistic mad painting – this one is a picture of my jazz man!"

SCHOOL

"I liked religious education because the teacher was really funny. He was the coolest teacher in the whole school. He reminded me of Mr Bean because he used to pull funny faces in class. I was good at English – I've still got some wicked stories and poems that I wrote when I was younger. I used to spend hours on them. I didn't really bother with maths and science and subjects like that, apart from science practical, when we got to use the bunsen burner. I probably daydreamed the most in history – about my dance classes and routines.

"I dislocated my knee twice at school, once in the middle of a dance class. It just popped out. I was screaming, 'Get it back in!' so loudly it echoed around the whole building. Luckily the ambulance came quite quickly. The other time it happened was during a performance, on stage in front of all the parents. I was doing a duet with Kerry that I'd choreographed using strobe light effects and we were wearing really cool trilbies. When my knee went, one of the teachers tried to lift me off stage, but he was really thin and couldn't manage it. It was a bizarre moment. I was told I would never dance again, but of course I did."

Danielle: *"At school, Mel worked hard in dance and music and drama, but she'd always come home laughing about being in trouble over something. She was the loudest in the class and the teacher said he was sometimes that far away from smacking her around the face. My mum and dad always used to argue about who would go to Melanie's open night, because they knew it wouldn't be good. Mum went once and Melanie had convinced her that this teacher was picking on her. Mum asked him if he was, and he said, 'Well, I can't help it. I just automatically shout at the loudest. I know it isn't just Melanie, but she's always the one we can hear from the corridor.'"*

HIGH SCHOOL FRIENDS

"My best friend Rebecca and I were inseparable. When anything happened to one of us, it always seemed to happen to the other one, too. For instance, once I dislocated my knee and then a couple of weeks later Rebecca dislocated hers. A few days later we went to a party. She still had plaster on and I'd just had mine taken off. We were at the top of the stairs messing around with some eggs and a guy said to Rebecca: 'If you dare smash that egg on my face, you and your friend are dead meat.' So of course she went ahead and smashed it on his head. As a result, we got chucked down the stairs, so we never went to parties after that."

Danielle: *"She used to take the mick out of my friends, so I didn't really introduce her to them. Whenever I had friends round I'd take them straight to my room and stay out of her way. Still, I got on with her friends. I always wanted to go everywhere with them, especially when they were going to town. But I'd never walk along with Melanie – her friends would always look after me."*

BULLYING

"I didn't have many enemies at school. There were some people I just never spoke to, though.

"My mother always taught us to fight our own battles and said that we would never learn to grow up if we didn't fend for ourselves. All the other kids' mothers would be down at the school complaining about this and that, but mine never used to."

Danielle: *"If I ever got bullied at school, she'd say I couldn't stick up for myself and try and make me fight her to make me tougher. But I couldn't fight her because I was so small compared to her. I knew that she would protect me if anything bad happened, though. One day some kids were calling me racist stuff in the street and she ran down with this big baseball bat. She didn't hit them, but it really scared them. Straight after she'd done something like that, I'd think: 'Oh yeah, I like my sister.'"*

EXAMS

"I was terrible at exams! I revised for dance, drama and music and part of my English, but I didn't bother with the rest. I didn't think there was any point. Still, my dad was so strict about education that if I didn't get better marks than the year before, my dance classes would be cut. So I had to revise for hours on end. Now I'm glad I did."

"Me looking serious, glamourous and sexy all at once. What talent!"

TEENAGER

"I was in a girl gang in my early teens. I'd nearly always be egged on to be bad by them, or I'd say: 'Right, come on, we're gonna do this!' I'd never do any of it by myself. We were all as bad as each other, really. It just depended on who had the guts to do it that day. It was give and take a lot of the time and I used to get it back quite a bit.

"I don't know if anyone found me scary at school. Some of them probably didn't like me and thought I was completely pathetic, but others did like me. I never had a fight, but people used to fight for me. I could never have the mickey taken out of me, and I got threatened a lot. My gang and I had to go up to the top bus-stop rather than the bottom one, to avoid getting beaten up.

"I grew up when I left school and went to college. That's when you start feeling a sense of your own responsibilities and realise you can't be like a kid anymore."

Danielle: *"I looked up to Mel – I always wanted to borrow her clothes and stuff like that. She was really good to me sometimes. I remember she once gave me her bikini top when she got a bra and I wanted one, too.*

"I think I'm a bit more sensible than she is. Some of the things she does just aren't very sensible. I thought she was stupid for not working at school. I used to listen to my dad talking to her about it, but in the end he gave up. He gave up on me as well, although he was a lot stricter with her than he is with me.

"She never, ever babysat me because we'd end up arguing and I'd then run to my neighbour's house, crying. I used to get her back when she was about 15 and started sneaking out to nightclubs. She'd do her hair, then tie it back and pretend she was going to bed. As soon as my dad went to work, she'd get up, get ready and my mum would drop her off at a club. If she'd done anything bad to me that day, I'd tell my dad she'd been out and she'd get in loads of trouble. I never got my mum into trouble about it, though – just Melanie. She'd get grounded then. So the day she was going out she was usually lovely to me, so that I wouldn't tell."

LEFT
"Messing about with wigs in my wannabe model phase."

BOYFRIENDS

"The idea of losing your virginity was disgusting to me. For ages, even if I fancied someone at school, I'd never let it be made known.

"I had a crush on a guy called Spud though, and went out with him for a bit, but then I chucked him and was really horrible to him for some reason. I used to think boys were disgusting. Later I started going out with older boys who had cars and dropped me off at school. That was much better."

Danielle: "We never talked about stuff like boys together. When she brought her boyfriends round I got a bit jealous, and I didn't like any of them. I'd be really annoying and get in the way. At one point we shared a bedroom and I would never leave her alone with a boyfriend."

FASHION

"My best friend Rebecca and I always wore the same clothes, until we were 14 or 15. At school we wore really short skirts with black tights or black trousers and Wallabies. We both had our hair in a big bun and kiss curls, or all up with curls down on special days (if we fancied somebody)."

"This is me winning the sack race at a school Sports Day. This was one of the things I looked forward to every year."

Victoria

~

"About to climb the stairs. Showing my knickers, with a cheeky little smile and nice legs. Not much has changed, only now I wear a G-string!"

~

"Looking like a baby owl! Very young and dressed like a meringue. My nose hasn't changed."

~

"Am I drunk here? Nice chair, nice jumper and feet in perfect first position."

~

"Sitting on a wall in my back garden looking stunned. Lovely socks, but what *is* that on my head?! Thanks for my stylish dress sense, mum!"

~

"In my back garden, very young! Looks like I had a little more cellulite as a baby than I do now. Was I wearing socks or is that just my chunky, wrinkly ankles?"

EARLIEST MEMORIES

"My first memory is of my teddy, which an aunt and uncle bought for me when I was born. It was a really shabby-looking thing, but I loved it and wouldn't go anywhere without it. It got so dirty that my mum had to wash it in the washing machine. But I made such a fuss when it was taken away that in the end she got another teddy and pretended it was the same one until the other one was clean. I fell for it, even though they didn't look remotely alike. I must have been so gullible."

CLOCKWISE FROM TOP LEFT

~

"Taken in a sink at my house when I was very young."

~

"In my back garden – nice dress but obviously a very ugly age for me!"

~

"I look dead here! But cute, with a nice double chin. I look like I've just broken out of an egg."

~

"Me with my lovely sister Louise and brother Christian. I don't know the name of the one at the back with the big ears."

FAMILY

"There was a time when my sister Louise and I didn't get on at all. We never physically fought, but it used to really upset my mum and dad because we'd argue all the time over absolutely everything and couldn't even bear the sight of each other. But it's nice now because we really appreciate each other and she's probably my best friend. We share a lot of things and go out together whenever we can.

"I think I must have been a bit jealous because Louise had loads of friends and boyfriends and was always really popular. She had a boyfriend before I did. She even had one at primary school. Once some bloke turned up at the house and I really teased her about it: 'Surely that's not your boyfriend, his clothes are appalling!' I was always too embarrassed with boys to think about having a boyfriend.

"I had a blue *Fame* outfit and Louise had a red one. She always looked like the dweeby sister in it. One day we delivered something to a friend's house, where there were loads of dogs. My sister was pretty small, freckly and pale, with long red hair and she was wearing a red tracksuit with a red polo neck, red legwarmers and red jazz shoes. We dropped her off to put something through the letterbox while mum and I were turning the car around and she was gone quite a while. Suddenly, we saw about three big Red Setters running up to her and trying to mate with her. They thought she was a Red Setter, too, because she was all in red. She screamed and screamed!"

HOME

"I shared a bedroom with my sister for ages and then I got my own room. It was very girlie – white wallpaper with pink stripes and a dado rail round the middle, a pink carpet and a pink and white lace-covered bed."

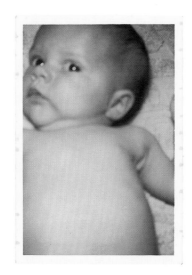

MY BIG SISTER, VICTORIA
by Louise Adams

"When my mum gave birth to my brother 18 years ago, Victoria was hysterical for days because she wanted a sister. I think she even had to come home from school because she was so upset about having a brother. I think she likes him now, though.

"We went to the same junior and senior schools. Nobody ever really thought of us as sisters because we didn't look alike and we were very different. Victoria was a model pupil and I wasn't. I liked being naughty – she was a teacher's pet.

"I felt sorry for her, because I had loads of friends and she didn't. Still, I looked up to her, too. She was always the best at dancing and singing and I was proud of that. I was never jealous, though, because I never wanted to do those things.

"It probably helps to be different. It would be more difficult if you were into the same things and wanted to do the same things.

"We got on okay, but we used to argue a lot, like sisters do – over things like me wanting to borrow her clothes and never giving them back. When I was very little I used to hit her. I always remember when we were sitting on the stairs at home and for some reason I turned around and smacked her. I think I was just being spiteful. My dad always said that if anyone hits you, you should hit them back, so she hit me. But my dad only saw her hitting me, so then she got told off. I said it wasn't my fault!

"She always said she wanted to be a singer or a dancer on telly, ever since I can remember. I didn't think she ever would, though. I used to say, 'yeah, yeah', but I didn't really take any notice."

MY BIG SISTER, VICTORIA
by Christian Adams

"When I was born, Victoria was upset because she didn't want a brother. I tell her that she already had a sister, so she had to have a boy. I never thought she didn't like me, though. My mum told me that when she was pregnant with me Victoria used to talk to my mum's tummy.

"When Victoria and I were sitting down watching telly, she always made me run up to her bedroom and get things for her. Sisters do, don't they? She also used to dress the dog up in shorts and a t-shirt. I fought with both my sisters a couple of times, about silly things. I can't remember what they were. Victoria never really hurt me physically, although I think Louise did a couple of times. Victoria was more gentle.

"We like the same music, but not the same food, because she doesn't eat loads of things. She's a fussy eater. I used to tease her quite a bit. She'd get up hours before going to school so she could do her hair and make-up and all the things girls normally do. I just used to get up five minutes before we had to go, have a wash, get dressed and still be in the car before she was.

"We're fairly close now. I feel as though I could take a problem to her if I needed to. If I had a problem with a girl, for instance, I think I would probably ask her advice. I think I'd talk to both sisters about it, really."

NAUGHTY GIRLS

"Once my dad bought a brand new van and we'd just had a brand new wall built. Me and my brother and sister got in the van and I knocked the handbrake off, so it rolled down the drive and smashed the brick wall in. Brand new van, brand new brick wall – my dad went absolutely ballistic. And I blamed it all on my little brother!"

FEELING SICK

"When I was really young my parents thought I had meningitis, but it turned out to be a very bad case of flu. Then when I was seven I had really bad tonsilitis and couldn't breathe. I was rushed into hospital, which was pretty horrible. I had repeating glandular fever as well – sometimes I think I've still got it. Actually I don't know if it's glandular fever or I'm just a bit tired."

FIRST FRIENDS

"When I was really young I had a friend called Douglas whose parents were friends with my parents. He used to come round and make me dress him up in girl's clothes. Douglas was always the girl, so he'd be the princess while I was the dwarf or the jester or something really stupid. He made us call him Charlotte. I didn't enjoy dressing him up – he was just very dominating. If we were playing animals, he'd say: 'You be the horse and I'll be the rabbit.' He wanted the girlie part every time and always gave me the boring part.

"I didn't have an imaginary friend but I always wanted a miniature person I could put in my pocket and carry around with me. At one point I had hardly any friends at all, so I used to hang around with my sister and all her friends. It was probably really annoying for her to have me there all the time."

"Yes, the press rumours are correct. Posh Spice views her new property!"

POP STARS

"The first band I ever really liked was Bucks Fizz, who did a dance routine where the men ripped the skirts off the girls. My mother made me one of these skirts and I'd do the dance in the playground with my sister. There'd be a particular moment when I'd say: 'Right, rip the skirt off now.' I'd be giving it like an absolute idiot."

Louise: *"We used to dance to Buck's Fizz all the time – I was one of the men. My mum even made Victoria one of those skirts that you can rip off. She used to get all the fancy outfits and I'd get all the boring ones or I'd have to be the man. I wasn't happy about that. I didn't like* Fame *much, but she did. She had* Fame *everything – the tracksuit, bags, sticker albums – everything you can think of. She also loved Bros and Five Star, but we weren't allowed to put posters on our wall."*

Victoria: "I was a real Bros fan and had the stars and stripes jeans they wore. I remember screaming and going absolutely mental at one of the concerts because I was convinced I was going to marry Matt Goss. All I did was think about him. I was so obsessed that it was ridiculous. I remember crying to my mum: 'I've got to meet him. You've got to tell me a way to meet him.' I was a nutter about the whole thing. I forgot all about it until we had an interview with *The Face* and I was asked who my favourite band was when I was young, and said Bros. I said I loved Matt Goss, because with his spiky hair he looked like a baby duck that had just broken out of an egg.

"One day when we were on the film set, Jenny, our hairdresser, went over to the pub. Her husband used to work with Matt Goss and, unbelievably, he walked into the pub after her and they had a chat. She explained that she was doing the Spice Girls' hair and he said: 'One of them is really cute. I really like her and she mentioned in an article that she used to fancy me. Can you arrange for me to meet her?' I don't still fancy him, but I would love to have met him for my own satisfaction. I was gutted that we were too busy and I didn't have time to go over. But I thought it was a really nice way to round off the whole Matt Goss episode in my life. I couldn't believe it, really. If I'd have thought all those years ago that Matt Goss might want to meet me some day…"

TELEVISION

"I loved a kids' show called *Emu's House*, with Emu, Rod Hull and big fat Grotbag. Every time a bell rang, a group of young stage school kids would come on dancing and singing: 'That's the doorbell! That's the doorbell!' I'd sit there thinking: 'I want to be one of those dancers.' They looked really cool and wore bright shorts and bright tops and far too much make-up.

"I've never really watched TV, though, because I haven't got the concentration. I loved *Fame*. I liked *Grange Hill* even though I hardly ever watched it, but I always watched *Top of the Pops*."

SINGING AND DANCING

"My sister came along to dancing lessons with me and we used to do choreography competitions together. Once we did one with her friend Alison and my friend Lorraine – the four of us did a tap dance to *Wash That Man Right Out Of My Hair*. Three of us were quite good at dancing, but my sister had two left feet. I used to shout at her because she could never get the tap dance right and was always trailing behind. But because she was my sister she had to do it with me.

"If I didn't get the main part in the play at school, I'd make sure I opened the show with a dance. Once when we did *Frosty the Snowman* and I didn't get the main part, I put up my hand and said: 'I have to be *Frosty the Snowman* because my mum's got the outfit.' They asked me to take it in the next day to show it to them, so my mum was up making pom-poms all that night.

"At junior school my teacher, Mrs Harvey, helped me get used to performing in front of audiences from an early age. No one ever did any work after lunch because she'd get me to do a dance on the carpet, with everyone sitting there watching me. I'd get up there and improvise a dance out of *Fame*. I was convinced I was Coco, even though I was completely the wrong colour and not half as good. I used to force the splits to try and copy her."

Louise: *"When she was at junior school, she always had to be the main part in the school play, or she wouldn't be in it. At that age, not many of the kids have got talent, so the teachers used to say that whoever had the outfit for the main part could play it. Victoria always put her hand up and said: 'Yes, I've got the Pied Piper's costume at home.' She once told everyone she already had the outfit for* Frosty the Snowman *and Mum had to make it for the next day. One year she couldn't be the main part, because it was for a boy, so she had to open the school play by doing a dance from* Fame. *She always wanted to be in the limelight."*

LEFT
"Me and Louise all dressed up ready for a little dance class show."

SCHOOL

"I was never really into science or English, and was never particularly good at anything, but I loved art. I was going to do A-level art at night school a couple of years ago and Geri was going to do Spanish, but things got too busy. I had a really nice art teacher at school and I liked my history teacher, too. I wasn't very good at history but I liked it because he was such good fun. I had a very sexy maths teacher. He was the PE teacher as well and he'd come in every day dressed in tiny shorts, showing his long footballer-type legs. When you're about 15 and you see this blonde, blue-eyed pair of legs running around, it's not very easy to concentrate! I had to make sure my maths stayed at the same standard so that I wasn't dropped or put into a higher class. I couldn't get too good or I'd have to leave his class.

"I really suppressed myself at school. If I were to go back now I wouldn't do my homework. I wouldn't be dominated by teachers telling me what to do and would probably be really naughty. Even though everyone thinks I'm really quiet and I never do anything wrong, at the end of the day I've got a wicked streak."

Louise: *"She had a bad time at senior school. I used to have to stick up for her, even though I was younger. If someone in my year had a brother or sister in her year, I used to say to them: 'She's not as bad as you think.'*

"People didn't like her because she didn't go out every night and hang around street corners, smoking. She used to go to a lot of singing and dancing lessons, so she didn't really socialise with them. The fact that my dad took us to school in a Rolls-Royce didn't help. Everyone thought she was a different class to them, and people don't like that when you're younger. They think everybody should be the same.

"She really liked her history teacher and her maths teacher. I used to tease her for doing her school work because I never saw the point in it. She used to say that you have to do it – you're supposed to do it.

"She used to go out with the friends she did have at lunch time, to keep out of everybody's way, so I didn't see her much at school. Anyway, I was probably smoking with a kid behind the bicycle sheds."

RIGHT
"All the Adams kids with their proud father back in 1982."

EXAMS

"I got really nervous before exams because, although I didn't want to do anything academic in the end, I always wanted to please my mum and dad and do the best I could. I never wanted to look back and think I should have tried harder. But I haven't got a lot of concentration so, instead of reading plays like *Romeo and Juliet* for English, I'd get the video out. I've got a photographic memory, which helped.

"My French oral exam was quite funny. We had to make a speech, and went in individually. Because I knew loads of the people who'd been in before me, I figured out that I'd be asked to speak about one of about four or five subjects. So I worked out a big long talk that could have fitted any of the subjects and crammed it with loads of really impressive phrases like 'combine harvester'. I think I said that the weekend before I'd been into the countryside and ridden horses and had a go on a combine harvester. I also said that the stock exchange really interested me. The speech was about three pages long and I learnt it all by heart. My examiner just stood there with her mouth open. Afterwards she came up to me and said: 'I don't know how you did it, but I take my hat off to you!'

"My worst exam experience was a biology mock. The exam paper wasn't very clear because it was from the year before and the pages were creased. It asked, 'What is menstruation?' But I couldn't read it properly and thought it said, 'What is constipation?' So I wrote a great long essay about constipation being when you can't go to the toilet. Imagine what the teacher must have thought!"

BULLYING

"I hated a lot of people in my class purely because they all hated me. Some of them used to wait for me outside the school gates to beat me up and I had to get teachers to walk me out in case I was attacked.

"One time I had a crush on a boy called Glen, big time. I look back now and think he was an ugly git, but I really liked him then. His girlfriend and her friends waited outside the school gates one day to beat me up because I fancied him, even though there's no way he would ever have fancied me. She used to pick on me a lot.

"I saw her a little while ago working behind the reception desk at the local sports centre and thought: 'Huh! You can have Glen now, mate. I don't need him.' It's really funny when you see people like that and they try and be all friendly to you while you're just thinking: 'You made my life hell and I used to cry because of you.' I'd love to be shut in a room with all those people now. I wouldn't be horrible, I wouldn't say anything and they'd just feel ridiculous."

Louise: *"I don't think she was bullied that badly. She got a bit of verbal abuse, but it wasn't anything major. The people who picked on her were often friendly to me, which was odd. I was the mouthy one and I didn't mind mouthing off to older people, but Victoria was quite shy."*

TEENAGER

"I used to hate being called Vicky. It was always Victoria. I think it was because I knew someone called Vicky who made me feel sick every time I thought of her. I hate Vic. If anyone calls me that, I ignore them. The Girls sometimes call me that, but most of the time they call me Tor, which I prefer.

"My sister was a lot cleverer than I was, but she just didn't bother to do as much work at high school. I worked hard but I still did a lot of daydreaming about performing. I always wanted to sing and perform, but I never knew how to make it happen."

Louise: *"I used to feel I was very different to her, because I wanted to go out all the time and stay out all night and she didn't. She did her homework and I didn't. My parents accepted us for who we were and never pressured me into doing mine, but Victoria would always want to do hers because she wanted to be in the teacher's good books.*

"As we were getting older I started looking up to her more. I was growing up and realising how horrible I used to be to her. I was an awful teenager but by the time I was 15 and Victoria was 18 we were getting on a lot better, even though we were still arguing every now and then."

GET A JOB

"If I wanted something, my mum and dad never just used to go and get it for me, even though they were quite well off. I'd have to wait for my birthday, or a special occasion. I had a Saturday job for a very short time. A friend of my mum and dad owns a wedding shop and I worked in there on the till and messed everything up. I couldn't bear it. So she gave me a job modelling in a fashion show instead. Walking up and down wasn't quite so taxing!"

"Me and Louise being forced to pose in front of the Rolls-Royce I never wanted to go to school in. I don't have any problems with a nice Roller these days!"

FASHION

"I've always liked clothes and used to nick my sister's all the time. It was great when I was old enough to get the train into London by myself and buy something to wear for Saturday night. I went to Warehouse a lot, although I hate to admit it now. In fact, I went to all the usual high street stores, but I was always really fussy.

"At school we had a choice between a kilt and a grey skirt. I went for the grey skirt in a very small size so it fitted me like a pencil skirt, which was quite cool. I had a white shirt and an extremely skinny stripey tie, which was the trendy way to have it. My blazer was huge, because at the time it was trendy to wear everything in a big size. I wore socks that came above the knee and started off a trend of wearing one pair of socks pulled up really tight and another pair on top all wrinkled down, so I had more wrinkles than everybody else. I always had a nice school bag."

Louise: *"Victoria always looked very smart in her school uniform. Her skirt would always be the right length. Mind you, she'd always have a full face of make-up on and have her hair done. It took her ages to get ready in the morning. She used to get up about two hours before she went to school and my dad was always waiting to give her a lift, shouting, 'We're late!' She's always been the same. I don't think she did PE at school because she didn't want to mess up her hair and make-up. My mum used to write letters for her so she didn't have to do it.*

"When Victoria was about fifteen she started going out in the evenings, with her friend at school, Sarah. They used to go to a place called the Ritzy in Tottenham, wearing funny-coloured tights and hotpants. My mum and dad would pick her up outside the night club at about 4am. She didn't like that at all, but they wouldn't let her get a bus home. I was usually asleep in the car when they picked her up."

RIGHT
"A bit of a bad dress day, but it doesn't hurt to experiment!"

LEFT
"In the study at home, aged about 16, getting ready to go to a dinner and dance (nice!) with my boyfriend, who is cut out of the picture because he's so disgusting – not just in looks, but as a person, too! *Nice perm!* There goes any fashion credibility I had!

BOYFRIENDS

"I didn't have a boyfriend at school. I was always so busy going to dancing classes that I didn't have time for them, and no-one fancied me anyway. I had crushes on loads of people, but none of them were interested in me."

Louise: *"I had boyfriends at play school, junior school and all through senior school. I was definitely the rebel out of the two of us. She probably had boyfriends at school that she didn't tell me about, but I don't remember any. I never used to see her in the holidays – she was always at dancing lessons.*

"When she was 18, Victoria had one of her boyfriends – Mark – come to live with us because he didn't get on with his own mum and dad and had nowhere else to go. I didn't like him in the beginning. We didn't get on at all. I didn't want him in the house, so I made it difficult for him and we used to shout at each other all the time. I just didn't like walking into the lounge and finding someone who wasn't my family sitting there.

"Victoria used to get annoyed, but she didn't really get involved. She kept out of it, so it didn't come between us too much. My mum used to try and sort it out, but I even moved out for a few days because I didn't get on with him. In the end, I started making an effort with him because he was there and there wasn't a lot else I could do. I ended up quite liking him, but I thought he wasn't right for Victoria. He was plodding along in life and she wanted more out of life than he did."

"Singing along with my dad to Stevie Wonder's *Sir Duke*. A natural!"

Mel C

ALBUM: CLOCKWISE FROM TOP LEFT

~

"My school photo in the first year of high school. You can see my gym leotard under my shirt, 'cos every lunch and break I'd be down the gym, practising my tumbles... pooh, smelly!"

~

"Me and two of my bestest pals at a dancing competition. We won a trophy for first place in a modern trio to the music of *Hill Street Blues*. I've got my favourite LFC trackie on! I think I was about twelve."

~

"A day trip out when we were on holiday in Menorca. Who's the cool dude in the shades? Never seen her before in my life!"

~

"Me in the juniors, proud with my gymnastics trophy and medals. Floor was my favourite apparatus – that's where I first learnt to do a backflip!"

~

"Sporty Spice! Well, I think pool's a sport. This was on holiday in Sussex, where some of my family live. That's my cousin Sean – sorry, mate! Is that a pair of **braces** I've got on?"

~

"Another dancing comp – me, Ali and Steph. We're all about 13 or 14, getting ready for our ballet trio, *Greensleeves*."

~

"When I was about 14 I went on a dance course in Menai, North Wales. All my mates were there. Zoë, on the far right, is Christine in *Phantom of the Opera* in the West End now – she's got a phenomenal voice."

EARLIEST MEMORIES

"Some of my very early memories are of Christmas, when my parents were still together. I was about two or three, and I got this wicked, Tudor-style dolls house which had a red roof and a removable back so you could play with everything inside. I got a really good doll's buggy, too, which I loved.

"Another Christmas, when my parents were divorced, I went to stay with my Dad. He got me this doll that ate and then pooed, which sounds really gross now, but was great at the time. It had little sachets of food that you mixed up and fed it. Then you stroked its belly and poo came out, so you had to change its nappy."

ABOVE
"My brother Paul looking rather handsome in his new car, outside our new house. He's the best brother you could wish for – he's one of my best mates. All my mates fancy him, but they know he's out of bounds!"

BELOW
"Paul again, on holiday with me – a little younger, but just as cute."

MY LITTLE BROTHER, PAUL

"My brother and I had a very loving friendship but we still used to fight. We'd roll about on the floor and pull each other's hair. He used to break everything I had."

MY BIG SISTER, MELANIE
by Paul O'Neill

"When our Mel was younger, my mum couldn't pay for her singing and dancing competitions and my child allowance used to be put with hers to help with the costs. I didn't know about it, but I wouldn't have minded if I had.

"My dad was a taxi driver, but he and I were in a crash in 1985 and that wiped us out because he then spent all his money on a new car that was a bit of a heap, so he had his hand in his pocket all the time. The crash was pretty bad – Mel was distraught because it was touch-and-go with my dad. He was badly hurt. I remember Mel and my mum stayed in my hospital room the night it happened. I couldn't sleep on my own for a while after the accident, so Mel and I shared a room. We slept in bunk beds and every night before we went to sleep we'd sing songs. She liked Madonna and Bros and was into Bruce Willis, too. She loved that song Under the Boardwalk. We always used to sing ourselves to sleep, which was dead nice and dead funny.

"I suppose Mel was a bit of a tomboy, because she always had lots of mates who were lads. They were really good fun and I used to mess about with them quite a bit. She always gets on well with lads and I get on really well with girls, probably because I grew up with a really nice sister. I was always able to talk to her, and as a result I've always respected other girls."

"Me, Paul and my mum all dressed up at a family dinner – I think it was my grandad's retirement when I was about 16."

NAUGHTY GIRLS

"I can't remember getting into trouble much when I was younger, but I did give my mum a lot of aggro when we'd left my dad. He'd bought me this little fluffy dog and it was the only thing I had that reminded me of him. I used to grab it and hug it, and when I was having a tantrum I'd lie on the couch and bang my legs, shouting, "I want my dad!" It must have been really horrible for my mum. I ran away a couple of times, as everyone does at that age, but I'd always be back about an hour later to have my tea.

"When I was in junior school we put an upturned drawing pin on somebody's chair and the teacher went ballistic. When she explained how out of order it was, we felt really bad.

"I told a fib about rollerboots once. I only had the skates at first, but I used to say that I had a pair of rollerboots that my Mum wouldn't let me wear, because they were too good. Then one day the girl from across the road came over and said: 'Where are your rollerboots, then?' in front of my mum. I was devastated. I've never lied again because I was so mortified. In the end I got some skates, but they were crap. Still, there was a really good smooth path on the corner of the house opposite and we used to skate up and down there."

HOME

"From the age of about three to eight we lived in very rough areas on council estates. Then we moved to Widnes and got our own house, but it was next to a lot of council flats and quite rough. I didn't realise until I was older that all my friends lived in nice areas and I lived literally on the other side of the tracks, over the Bongs, which was the rough area.

"My mum never had very much money. When we moved into our first house, my bedroom had *Magic Roundabout* wallpaper on one wall and we had it there for years. It was really embarrassing, because even when I was 13, I still had *Magic Roundabout* wallpaper. But now that would be well cool, wouldn't it? Eventually, one wall was papered with Pierrot the clown and I also had a Pierrot quilt. It was the pants and I loved it. I used to do really stupid things to my room like hang pieces of chiffon to the ceiling and have lengths of sequins coming down."

CHRISTMAS

Paul: *"Christmas wasn't great when we were young because we didn't have a lot. It was always the same – get up, open my presents, find out I didn't get what I wanted because they couldn't afford it, have a mess about with our Mel and then go to our nan's and grandad's."*

"Smile, everyone! This picture is of one of my older brothers, Jad, my step-dad, Paul, me and my mum. It was taken at Christmas '96 – *2 Become 1* was number one and on Christmas Day we all sat and watched *Top of the Pops*. My first Christmas being 'famous'!"

FIRST FRIENDS

"I had an imaginary friend, Bert, named after Bert and Ernie on *Sesame Street*. I saw him when I was about three and we were going over a railway bridge in the car. He was walking down the road and I shouted: 'Mum, mum, there's Bert!' She smiled and said, 'Yes', the way mums do. No-one believed me, but I know I really did see him. Recently, I bought Bert, Ernie, the Cookie Monster and some of the others from *Sesame Street* and *The Muppets*. Then last night I was lying in bed, sleeping and feeling dead comfy, and I reached over and grabbed one of my cuddly toys. I must have been dreaming about something, because when I woke up I was cuddling the Cookie Monster!

"I used to be friends with the other kids in our street. I particularly remember Diane from across the road. She was my best friend and she was gorgeous. I was a fat, plain, tubby, frumpy kid with a little brown bob, and she had really tanned skin, blue eyes and golden hair. We used to put her hair in rags every night so that she could have ringlets, but I couldn't have them because my hair was in a pageboy style. Looking back now I think I looked cute, but at the time I thought I was ugly and she was gorgeous.

"We used to play out in the street a lot with dolls, even as I got older. I had about 15 Sindy dolls, all with different-coloured hair – I made their clothes and gave them haircuts. I played in the park a lot – we used to teach each other loads of tricks on the bars, spinning round on your leg, sitting up with no hands and hang-swing-drops."

FAVE GAMES

"At junior school we played handstands against the wall, British Bulldog and Stuck In The Mud. We all had recorders and even though we couldn't play them, we'd run up and down the playground blowing them. I played football with my brother. I wanted to be a goalie – Bruce Grobbelaar, in fact."

FOOD

"Chinese was always my favourite food. My Mum and Dad took me to Chinese restaurants, even when I was really young, and I always loved hot, spicy things like curry, too."

TELEVISION

"*Top of the Pops* was my favourite TV programme. I used to watch *Dallas* with my Mum and I really liked Pam Ewing. I loved *Charlie's Angels* when I was really young, and had loads of *Charlie's Angels* gear. I liked the one with the dark hair who wasn't the tomboy. Now I like *Brookside* the best and *Eastenders*, but I watch *Coronation Street*, too. We miss a lot of TV when we're away, but you can always keep up with the soaps. Soaps keep my feet on the ground. I know all the characters, so it's like something to come home to."

POP STARS

"I loved dressing up when I was quite a bit younger. I'd either dress like a showgirl, or Madonna. I thought I was Madonna for ages and when I was a bit older I thought I was Neneh Cherry. I put loads of posters on my wall – Bruce Willis, Adam Ant, Cory Haim and Madonna, of course. I even went through a phase of thinking Kylie Minogue was really cool – not in the *I Should Be So Lucky* stage, but when she went all trendy."

TOP
"Me and my best friend Alison, dressed up in our ballet duet costume – it was called *Minuet* and we were *en pointe*. Looking good!"

ABOVE
"Me and Alison at a dancing show. We were about 12 and just about to go on for *Viva España!*"

SCHOOL

"My favourite subject at school was PE. I did loads of gymnastics and I played centre in the netball team. I used to play hockey, too, but I was rubbish at it. I was quite good at French, and maths was my worst subject. I didn't really like sciences, either. I really enjoyed drama and I was in all the school plays. I was in *Annie*, and in *The Wiz* I played one of the crows and the messenger. In *Blood Brothers* I played Mrs Lyons, the posh woman. It was a really good part, but I wanted to be the scouse mum. I was in the school choir as well, so I was quite in with the music department."

Paul: *"Mel used to work hard at school. She was really clever, but I often saw her crying because she couldn't do her homework as well as she wanted to. Once she couldn't do the last bit of this piece of homework she had. It was a drawing of a 3D car and she said it didn't look right, but it looked spot on to me. She's always been a perfectionist, and still is. I remember when we were on holiday in the Caribbean and I said, 'Just have a chip. Let me see you eat a chip!' but she was having none of it. She's really into healthy eating. She's probably the fittest person in Widnes. She's full of muscles. She's kicked my ass a few times and I wouldn't like to have a fight with her. But, then, even my mum can beat me in an arm wrestle.*

"She always backed me up when I was at school and gave me a hand with school work. She'd kept all her old school books, so she let me look at them, which really helped.

"When she was still at school doing her GCSEs, we went into a drama studio where Mel was recording a song with my mum's band. I was only 10, but I remember thinking it was mum singing because she was so good. I thought, 'She's amazing.' I joined her school the next year and all the music and drama teachers used to ask me about our Mel. They tried to force me into doing music because they thought I'd be as good as she was. I joined the choir for a few months. I wasn't bad, actually, but then my voice started to break and I sounded like a twit."

GREATEST DANCER

"I would spend all day Saturday at the dancing school at the bottom of the town. I used to get the bus there and walk home if my mate's mum didn't give me a lift back. We'd start at nine and get home about five. I did ballet, modern, and national dancing mainly. I didn't do a lot of tap because I didn't like it that much. I used to go a couple of nights after school as well, from four to eight."

EXAMS

"I used to get very nervous about dancing exams, which we had every couple of months. I usually got highly commended and honours for them, though. For some of my other exams, I didn't revise until the night before and I really regretted it because then I sat in the exam room thinking: 'Oh no, I can't do it!' I did really well in my GCSEs, though. I got 4 Bs and 5 Cs. If I could go back to school, I'd take music in my options instead of cookery, which I had to do if I took drama. I changed to music in the fourth year, but I'd missed loads of work in the third year, which was annoying.

"With everything, I think that if you're going to do something, you should do it well. It frustrates me when I can't do things. I get really frustrated driving because, although I've passed now, I want to be a good driver, but I'm not because I've got no experience."

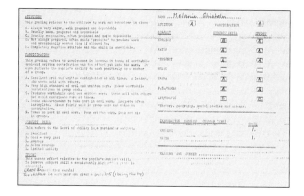

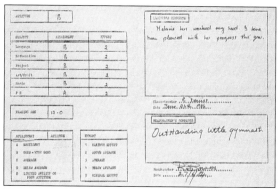

FAIRFIELD HIGH SCHOOL

BIRTHDAYS

"For my birthdays, my Mum always used to make an iced Victoria sponge cake, my nan and grandad would come down and I'd have a friend over. Mum made salmon and cucumber sandwiches on brown bread and we had crisps. We never usually had crisps or chocolate in the house, because they weren't a necessity. We didn't have grapes or anything like that. It was always just apples."

BULLYING

"One day I was in the fields at the back of the house. A girl was walking behind me with her cousin, following me home. I could hear them saying all this stuff about me and I thought, well, I'm not going to walk any faster because I'm not scared yet. I wasn't worried, because she'd never caused any trouble with anyone before. But then she came up behind me and grabbed my plait, bent me right back and started dragging me across the floor. I was so shocked that I didn't cry or anything. I just couldn't believe it and she couldn't believe that I wasn't crying. I got up and they started whacking me around the head, but then a lad came over and stopped it."

Paul: *"I remember, once, at the end of her fifth year at school, when she'd just been made a prefect, she came home crying. She'd been beaten up by some silly girls who were jealous of her because she was so talented. It happened in the field near our house, so I went over there on my bike, looking for them, but I didn't find them. I was fuming."*

FRIENDS

"It was really horrible because my best friend from junior school just turned against me in the last two years of high school. It was weird because I'd been really good friends with her and her sister and cousin, but that suddenly changed and they hated me. I think it was partly because I was going out with a lad who she'd been out with years before and I think she still liked him. And the girl I then became best friends with (because we had a lot of similar interests) was originally her cousin's best mate. So that turned her against me. I was friends with all her family until she told her parents that I'd been saying nasty things about them. And I'd never do that because I've been brought up not to do anything like that.

"I had quite a few best friends. A girl called Clare was my best friend in junior school. My best, best friend is a girl called Alison and I still see her today. She's one of my dancing friends. I spent so much time at dancing classes when I was younger that I got to know a whole separate group of friends outside school."

Paul: *"I really liked two of her school mates, Alison and Rachel, and they're still her mates now. But some of the others were really awful. They used to rip me to bits because I was Mel's younger brother. She used to swear and I blackmailed her over it, so she said: 'If we both swear, then neither of us can tell Mum on the other.' I thought that was a really good idea. She wasn't a goody-two-shoes, but she wasn't ever nasty either."*

FASHION

"There was a toy shop in Widnes called Toy Master. My mates and I would go in there but we could never buy anything. I spent all my money on dancing, which meant that I couldn't have many clothes or toys. I hardly ever had any clothes – just my school uniform, a pair of jeans, a few sweatshirts and that was it. My Dad bought me clothes when we went away, but that wasn't very often. I used to babysit for our Paul to earn extra money. I got two pounds a night.

"I went through a phase at school when I was 15 of wearing really short skirts. I also wore big long socks pushed down and nurse's shoes with red ribbons instead of laces. Out of school I thought I was really cool wearing baggy, ripped jeans. At the disco, everyone used to take the piss out of me, but I thought I was dead cool."

"Uh-oh – fashion disaster! This was taken at Christmas 1988 and I'm posing with my new keyboard. Nice perm, nice suit, nice *curtains*!"

TEENAGER

"In my teens, I went through a stage of thinking I didn't belong anywhere. We went to live with my nan for a little while until my mum got herself together after the split with my dad, and then we got a council flat in Runcorn, which was horrible. My Mum and Dad's divorce affected me in my teens quite a lot, but I still think I was lucky in a way that it happened so early. A friend of mine's parents split when she was 16 and that really messed her up. It's funny when you get to puberty, because your head just goes wet. My Mum was remarried and had my little brother, so they were a little family. They used to go on holiday together, but I went away with my dad – so when I saw all their holiday photographs I used to think: 'They're a family, and although I'm a part of it, I'm also not a part of it.' When my Dad remarried and had a family, I thought, 'Well he's got his happy family, my Mum's got her happy little family and I'm just completely alone.' That was how I felt then, but now I feel lucky to have two families."

Paul: *"Our Mel and I didn't get on when we were younger. I was about 10 when she was going through puberty and I used to make her cry all the time. I was a bit overweight then and she used to call me 'anorexic' as a joke. I just called her 'pizza face'. When she had a lot of mates round the house and my mum and dad were out, I'd say, 'If you don't let me do this, I'm going to tell our parents you've had people here!' We had some great fights. Once, I hit her and she started crying, then she smacked me one back and near enough knocked me out. She's hard! But at the end of the day we were always there for each other."*

"Who's that poseur? Oh no, it's me! Nice shoulder pads. What's goin' on? I look like an extra from *Eldorado*."

BOYFRIENDS

"I went out with one lad at school for about three years – the class clown. He was really popular and I was very quiet. He always liked me but I didn't like him at first. I was a bit scared because he was so cocky and he went on about it really loudly. He used to write our names on the desk, which was a bit embarrassing. I finally fell for him, but in the end he finished with me and I was gutted. We're still good friends, though. I always see him when I go home."

Paul: *"Mel's first boyfriend was a lad called Tim. He's a nice lad – I still talk to him. I think our Mel finished with him on the stairs at our old house. I was laughing my head off, but he was really upset."*

SPOTS

"I never had bad spots, just teenage pimples. Every two weeks I'd get a great big one on my nose, but it wasn't really problem."

Paul: *"When I started getting spots and stuff, I suddenly realised how terrible I'd been to Mel in the past. When it happened to me, she could have ripped me to pieces like I did to her, but she didn't. She's that nice a person that she just helped me out with some spot cream, instead."*

"Ooh, Mel, you're so trendy. It's me again on holiday in Menorca back in '89, chillin' in the sun. Like the vest."

"The gang from my dancing school after we swept the board at the Regional Scholarship and Championships. I spent my life dancing – I loved it – but singing has always been my favourite thing. I could never believe it when we won things. I still can't."

Geri

ALBUM: CLOCKWISE FROM TOP LEFT

~

"The goofy sailor look.
I need a brace!"

"When I was about three
I decided to do a mini
fashion show in the back
garden with my dad
taking the pictures. I'm
not too happy here,
sweltering in my winter
collection!"

~

"Me and my big sister
Natalie showing off our
matching hair and
shorts in the back
garden."

~

"Blues Brothers on the
beach in Ibiza."

~

"Look what the cat
dragged in – me at about
ten years old."

~

"What a little angel!"

~

"An early swimsuit shot.
Bet *The Sun* would kill
for it."

EARLIEST MEMORIES

"My earliest memory is of being in my buggy and saying 'hello' to people on the other side of the road as I was being pushed down the street. One of my first words was 'actually' and everyone really laughed at me when I said it. And my nickname when I was very young was Cacitas, which means 'little poos' in Spanish, because I was always on the toilet."

FIRST FRIENDS

"I was friends with loads of kids in the street. I often played with a little Spanish boy up the road called Robert. We used to stare at Page Three together and giggle. I played Knock Down Ginger with the street kids and I was in a gang with my brother and friend, called the Daredevil Gang. We used to climb on the neighbours' roofs and then jump off them. One day I saw one of my neighbours naked while I was standing on his coal bunker.

"I often sat on the doorstep outside my house and wrote poems. I was very good at rhyming. In school, we all had to write our own little story and I created a character Mb out of two letters and a smile. After that, I began to see the letters everywhere and Mb became a kind of imaginary friend. It's funny to think that his initials were the same as Melanie Brown's."

MY BIG SISTER, NATALIE

"Natalie's naturally quite introvert but likes a giggle, and I'm very extrovert, so we were good partners in crime. We hung out together when my mum was at work – often we'd sing into our hairbrushes and pretend to be Abba and Wham. I was Natalie's little shadow most of the time. She's always been very protective of me, and she still is.

"When she started getting Saturday jobs I'd follow her everywhere she worked. She worked in a donut shop and I'd hang around outside. She worked in Chelsea Girl and I'd be in there all day. Everywhere she went, I went too. I even did half of her paper round for her. She used to get £1.25 for it – she kept the pound and I had 25p, even though I did just as much as her. We did a road each and I walked miles carrying a huge bag. I did it because I wanted to feel grown up, I suppose. I always spent the money on sweets and a magazine.

"My brother and I used to have a lot of fights and get quite aggressive with each other. He gave me dead legs the whole time and I bit his back and poked him in the eye. I wasn't as close to him then as I am now because there was quite an age difference between us."

ABOVE
"One of my first school pictures. I remember feeling disturbed that I hadn't known beforehand that it was 'photo day' so I didn't have my best dress on."

TOP LEFT
"Another outfit in my fashion show. Look at that golden glow around me – I was always going to be a star!"

BELOW
"Natalie and me on a 'toilet stop' when we were driving through the Pyrenees to our grandmother's house in Spain."

MY LITTLE SISTER, GERI
by Natalie Halliwell

"When she was born, Geri was like a new toy for my brother and me. My first memory of her is when my brother and I ran round and round her cot. She was inside, holding on to the bars and looking out with her big blue eyes, like a little caged animal.

"Max is the oldest – he's five years older than Geri. Max and I were best friends, but then Geri came along and I grew closer to her. Geri and I have been like a little partnership all the way through – a good team.

"We used to play dressing up for hours. We also played pop groups and used to put on family shows. Geri would do the singing, normally into a hairbrush, and I'd hum and play the guitar behind her. Our usual repertoire consisted of Abba songs.

"She's the youngest, so she's the one who gets spoilt and has her own way. That's why she's the way she is now. She's used to being the baby and getting away with murder. For instance, at school I always wanted to play lots of instruments, but my mum said no when it came to the violin because it makes a terrible noise when you're first learning. Yet when Geri wanted to learn to play the violin, she managed to get round my mum. She was always getting things that we hadn't been allowed.

"The only school we were both at was junior school. I remember being very protective because she's a bit of a loudmouth and the type of person who gets into trouble. She's a love-her-or-hate-her kind of girl. Some people thought she was a spoilt brat, but most people liked her because she was a character. She wasn't a quiet child and she'd always be singing and dancing for everyone.

"I remember times when she was getting on kids' nerves because she was such a little show-off and I'd stick up for her. There was one girl in my year who got her in the woods of our school and told her she was going to beat her up. I told my dad and he came up to the school to stop it."

HOME

"I shared a room with my sister, Natalie. It was quite messy, with loads of dollies everywhere. We used them to act out scenes in Dolly Land for hours and it was great when my dad made us a big dolls' house. We also had Legoland with Play People. Max and Natalie were Ernie and Lukey and I had to be John, the boring one, which I was a bit gutted about. Max had his own play land and made little characters out of socks by sewing eyes on them. They used to come into Dolly Land from time to time. I also had a Spanish doll called Nancy. She was like a big version of a Sindy doll – very sexy and pretty.

"My dad didn't work. It was only my mother who was working, so we didn't have much money. She was brilliant – she always fed us and made sure we were clean, with clean clothes. We were a bit jumbly, though. I remember a day at junior school when I peed myself and the teacher gave me a new pair of knickers to wear. I'd been wearing a really old pair with hardly any elastic, so I loved the new ones. They had fish on.

"I loved other people's birthday parties – playing pass-the-parcel and getting a goody bag when you went home. I felt a bit gutted because I was missing out, though, because my mum was a Jehovah's Witness when I was younger so we didn't celebrate birthdays or Christmas. I was the oddball, I was different, which was a bit upsetting. I don't really remember my birthdays because they just weren't an issue. I didn't start getting birthday presents until I was about 14, when my mother left the church, although I was given a pram when I caught nits once and had to have all my hair cut off.

"I thought everyone was better off than me. The grass is always greener, isn't it? I imagined they were all living a fantasy life with a perfect family and I'd sleep at their houses all the time. Sometimes I was sure I was adopted and my real princess mother would come and get me one day. Once I saw a picture of a model in C&A and thought: 'Yes, that's my real mother.'

"My mum used to take me from door to door saying 'The End Is Near' – that's what Jehovah's Witnesses do – and it was a bit embarrassing. We also used to have to sit quietly during hours of preaching sessions in Kingdom Hall, which is what the church was called, and that was murderous. I just played with my black dolly, Pippa. I took her with me everywhere.

"I had to go and live at my elder sister Karen's house when my parents were divorcing, so she was a bit of a surrogate mother to me for a while. I was about nine then and I think kids that age are quite adaptable in those circumstances."

"Dangerous Liaisons! Lady Geri, aged seven, giving it some in the school play."

"Aged 11. Dressed up in my school uniform for my first day at Watford Girls Grammar School. My cat, Carlos, is very proud."

OUR ROOM

Natalie: *"Geri and I used to share a room because we lived in a three-bedroom house. Max had the small room, my parents had the big room and Geri and I were in the middle room for years. We used to go to bed holding hands when we were little, because our beds were almost side-by-side. We'd say: 'Hold hands?', then stretch out and clasp each other until we fell asleep and our hands dropped to the floor. We talked a lot at night. We could change our beds over to bunk beds if we wanted, but I got a bit sick of that because Geri always used to sleep on top."*

FAVE GAMES

"I really liked this boy called Lee at junior school, who was the skinhead badboy of the class. All the girls fancied him, and I got to kiss him when we played True-Dare-Double-Dare-Love-Kiss-or-Promise, which was a top moment. We also played kiss-chase and hung upside down on the double bars to show the boys our knickers."

"Natalie used to work as a holiday rep in Ibiza. I was her shadow, so whenever I got the chance I'd follow her out there."

SINGING & DANCING

"One day I went to see my sister in the school play and another girl sang *I Wanna Be A Nightclub Queen*. I liked it so much that I picked up my sister's script and learnt the words. Around that time, I used to get up early and go with my mum to the library where she was a cleaner before I went to school. While she was hoovering I'd stand on one of the huge oak tables and sing into a big mirror. It was great because there was no one else there."

Natalie: *"Geri's had a good voice from the word go. Even though she was really tiny, she always had a deep, strong, husky voice. No one could believe the kind of voice that came out of such a little person and it was always a shock to people when she sang. Her favourite song was I Wanna Be A Nightclub Queen (the most famous ever seen) – she did that for everybody, from the age of about five onwards. Whenever we had guests round, Geri would do her party piece. No matter how many people were there, she'd always come down and do her thing in front of them all. She's always, always been a show-off."*

NAUGHTY GIRLS

"If we'd been naughty at all, I'd go up to my mum and ask: 'Who's been the goodest today?' I was indulged much more because I was the youngest, I suppose, and I got called 'spoilt brat' all the time. I think you get away with more when you're younger because your parents have been through all that with your brothers and sisters and they just say: 'Well, whatever…' when it comes to you.

"One day at infant school I hid in a tyre in the orchard and I stayed there so long that everyone came looking for me. I hid in the cloakroom another time, but no-one even noticed! I loved dressing up and going on adventures. I'd put on a miniskirt, take a handbag and wander off down the street."

Natalie: *"She was a very manipulative child. If we were naughty and she knew we were going to get into trouble, she would approach my mum and say: 'Mummy, I've been naughty. Do you want to smack me?' She would get there before my mum, and that way she'd be let off. It was all about reverse psychology."*

CHRISTMAS

"Because my mother was a Jehovah's Witness when I was younger and we didn't celebrate Christmas, it felt a bit weird at school because everyone else was celebrating and we weren't. I never believed in Father Christmas from the start, because no-one really told me about him."

"I wanna be a nightclub queen! Wrapped in a curtain – ever resourceful."

TELEVISION

"My favourite programmes were *Planet of the Apes*, *Space 1999* and *Think Again* with Johnny Ball. When I was little, I loved *The Magic Roundabout* and *Will o' the Wisp*. I watched quite a lot of telly when I was young. I loved old movies, like *Gone With The Wind* and *National Velvet*, and I'd often imagine I was Scarlett O' Hara or Elizabeth Taylor."

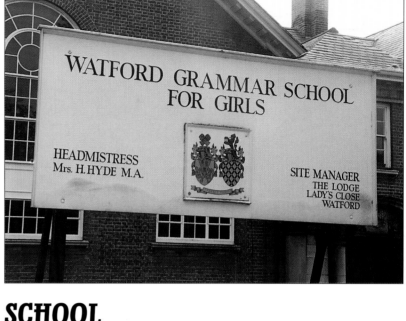

SCHOOL

"After junior school, I told my mum that I'd run away if she sent me to the same school as my brother and sister. It was so cool when I got the letter saying I'd been accepted at grammar school, especially when I found out that the vicar's daughter didn't get in, even though she'd gone on about how she was definitely going there.

"The school was very old and traditional, with the past headmistresses' portraits hanging on the walls. The kids there were very clever – real swots – and I was a fairly average student. I loved English literature and language and history, especially the 19th century and Tudor times. I wasn't interested in science. I couldn't see what relevance relativity or Newton had to my life.

"I think there should be classes in self-esteem and communication. Instead, in my first year, I had a teacher who said I was very lucky to be at the grammar, considering I came from a completely different background to the other girls. It was a bit snobby, but after the first year I broke through all that and got on well.

"If I went back to school now, I'd go in with different eyes. I'd pay attention in the lessons and probably give it a little bit more than I did. At 13, I became the class charity monitor. I tried to raise money for AIDS, which was a bit controversial at the time. There we were debating it and I was telling everyone it was an issue for them because they'd be having sex in three years time. After that, I became form monitor."

Natalie: *"Our local senior school had a bad reputation. They didn't push you and you weren't going to come out with any qualifications. I didn't want to go but mum said that because Max had, so would I, and all her kids got treated the same. But when it came to Geri, Mum decided that she was going to the girls' grammar, which was a really nice school in Watford that I would have loved to have gone to. To be fair, when she saw what it was like for Max and me, I think my mum decided that maybe we were right. Still, I was really annoyed about it. Geri got to go to the girls' grammar and have violin lessons."*

POP STARS

"I really loved Elvis. I thought he was so handsome and gorgeous."

Natalie: *"We both loved George Michael and Wham. We went to see them in concert when I was 15 and she was 12 and we were always buying George Michael posters. We both copied each other a bit – it went in phases. All my friends said that she copied me when she was little and when I started going out to discos she started dressing up as well. She loved slapping on loads of make-up and trying to act grown up. It used to be very upsetting for her when I went out in the evenings and she couldn't go too."*

BULLYING

"I didn't really have any enemies at school, although I was beaten up by one girl, who had it in for me for a while. We'd been friends before, but then she just turned on me. One day she picked up my comb and started combing another girl's really long greasy hair. Then she and a friend pinned me down and tried to get the comb through my hair immediately afterwards. As I was shouting, 'Get off!' she shoved the comb up my nose. We all ended up in the headmistress's office and I got in trouble, too, even though it wasn't my fault."

EXAMS

"Exams scared me quite a lot. Once I wrote all the answers on my legs just before I went into a music exam, but I bottled it and scrubbed them all off at the last minute. I was alright because I ended up remembering it anyway. I used to wing it a lot, especially in French and German, because I was quite good at them. I really fluked French. I didn't study for it, but I guess my Spanish helped. My Spanish isn't brilliant, but it's not bad.

"My mum didn't push me to do my homework. She left it up to me. If I was interested in something or I liked the teacher, I'd put my heart into it. If I didn't like it, I wouldn't give it one iota of attention. I went into loads of exams where I couldn't answer one question and just ended up writing stupid, silly answers and trying to be cheeky and funny. Which isn't clever."

TEENAGER

"When I was about 14, I kept lying to my mum about where I was going. I'd say I was going round a friend's house, but really we'd be hanging out in a park. Once my mum came to pick me up at the friend's house, but I wasn't there and she caught me running out of the park opposite. Another time I wasn't allowed out, so I sneaked out of the window. But when my friend dropped me off in the car later, the engine was roaring so loudly that my mum heard me as I came back in. As I was sneaking through the window, she grabbed me by the hair. It was terrible!

"I was always very cheeky and upfront. I remember debating work experience at school and, although I didn't know anything about it, I told everyone we had to go on strike to protest against it. I was always quite a domineering character, which sometimes got me into trouble. It either gets you liked or disliked, basically.

"In the first year of grammar school I was in *A Day In The Life Of Titch Oldfield*, as a little boy who was a good mimic and did impressions of Margaret Thatcher and Rene and Renata. The drama workshop closed down the next year and, although I did drama as a lesson, I only appeared in a couple of plays after that. All the other girls went to ballet and tap in their spare time, but I didn't because my mother didn't have the money to send me there and didn't believe in it all. She said: 'Sorry Geri, you can do all that when you're 16.'"

"I found out during an English literature class at college that my dad had died. I was gutted, but I tried to put a brave face on it. It was terrible because I was just developing a really close friendship with him. The last time I saw him was at my flat. I was playing a tune on the piano. It was terrible because it was so instant that I felt I'd never had the chance to say goodbye. At times like that you really need the rest of your family. When someone close to you dies, I think it makes you search even more to find out what the point is in living. Is it just a treadmill or is there a purpose to it all? I've explored lots of different faiths, like Buddhism and Spiritualism. You've got to have something or life becomes meaningless. I think the idea of reincarnation is very interesting. After all, if we all believed in it, we'd treat the world a lot better to make sure it was still there when we came back again.

Natalie: *"When we were younger, I gave her advice about boys and stuff. I've always told her everything. The first time I kissed a boy, the first thing I did when I came home was run straight upstairs to Geri and say: 'Guess what?*

I've kissed a boy!' And she said, 'Really? What was it like?' And I said: 'Oh, it's a bit slobbery, actually. I had to wipe my mouth with the back of my hand afterwards!' We've been lucky to be able to share all our secrets with each other.

"We've had some terrible fights, though – real physical fights – where we punch and hit each other. But we always make up the same day or, if not, the next day. The worst fight we ever had was when we were in Spain during festival time in August and Geri was 15 or 16. She was a bit of a wild child then – a bit uncontrollable. The two of us were out one night and we went to a bar where she fancied the barman. The only way she could get his attention was by ordering drinks. After a while we had about six beers lined up in front of us. She couldn't drink them, but she kept ordering more just so that she could speak to him. She kept telling him how much she fancied him, but he wasn't interested. So I dragged her out of there and told her to stop because she was acting like an idiot.

"She swore at me and stormed off back to my auntie's flat down the street. I walked home about 200 yards behind her and when we got there we had this massive fight, which Geri started. She waited until I was taking my jeans off and they were down around my ankles, so I couldn't move very well. Then she pounced on me and started hitting me. I hit her back and soon we were rolling around on the floor. She bit my calf really hard and drew blood and we tried to strangle each other. When Max came in, we were both lying on the floor, exhausted. He said: 'Oh my God, what the hell's been going on?' We were just black and blue."

HIGH SCHOOL FRIENDS

"My first best friend was Lorraine. We weren't allowed out at lunch time but we often sneaked out. We'd all want to go and get a burger but never had enough money, so I'd go around asking people for 10p and then get enough money together. I was the only one who dared to do that."

Natalie: *"Geri used to chop and change her friends a bit. Her best friend for a while was a girl called Lorraine, a much quieter girl than she was. I think Geri liked it because she could dominate her. Then, towards the end of school, she started hanging round with another girl called Charlotte, who was more confident and like herself. She always chose nice friends and never used to hang out with rough people. Geri had the kind of friends that my mum would approve of.*

"I've still got the same friends from school and they all know Geri from the days when she used to hang around with us. We had a standing joke that whenever I got a Saturday job they would semi-employ her as well, because she used to hang around me the whole time. When I was about 15 or 16, I got a job in a donut shop and she'd just come along and stay for most of the day. When I got my first paper round at 13, she used to do half of it for me."

BOYFRIENDS

"There was a boys' grammar near our school and we'd have discos together. I was really into make-up then and and I'd do all my friends up in pink eye-shadow and blue mascara and backcomb their hair before we went out. We met a group of boys there and began to hang out with them at weekends. All my friends were getting snogs, but I was so underdeveloped that the boys were just my friends. I didn't feel like going into a relationship, either, because I hadn't become aware of my sexuality."

Natalie: *"I had a pretty serious boyfriend in my late teens and that finished when I was about 20 or 21. Geri was about 17 and the rave scene had started, so I started hanging out with her and her friends. Our social circles kept crossing all the time and we even went out with the same guy – at different times, though. I went out with him and about three years later so did Geri. Neither of us had a serious relationship with him, so it wasn't a problem. When we see him now we still laugh and look at each other, saying, 'Quick! Do I look alright?'"*

FASHION

"I got told off all the time at school for rolling up my skirt and wearing black eyeliner and kitten heels. I first dyed my hair when I was 11, while my mum was out at work. I stupidly poured a bottle of peroxide on my head, which made my hair fall out. Still, it went a really nice blonde and I thought it looked great until I got dark roots."

GET A JOB

"My mother didn't give me any money – well, something like 50p a month – so I started working at about 13 or 14. I did loads of jobs – I was a waitress in Covent Garden at my friend's dad's restaurant, and worked on a market stall and in a fish and chip shop."

"Sweet but determined.
I always knew I'd be
a star one day!"

Spice Portfolio
#1

Wannabes

I'LL TELL YOU WHAT I WANT...

Once we found each other, we knew we had a future.
But there was a lot of hard work to put in before we got our
record deal and became the Spice Girls you know today...

LEAVING HOME

GERI: "I left home at 16 because I wanted my independence. Not long afterwards I had a party in the house I was living in. I went to this big pub called The Gamebird and invited everyone in there – 'Party at my house!' I had huge speakers in every room and a brilliant DJ. It was so ram-packed at one point that I couldn't even get inside my own house and there were people hanging out of the windows. It went on till three the next afternoon. Then I went to a rave from six in the morning to ten at night on the Sunday and started a job at a video company the next day!"

Natalie: "Our parents divorced when Geri was about nine and I was 12. After that my mum had this boyfriend and we didn't like him much. So we both left home as soon as we could, when we were 16. I went to work in Ibiza as a kiddie club rep and Geri rented a room in Watford.

"We've got an older step-sister called Karen and she owned a house which she and her husband had bought as an investment. They said to Geri that she could have a room at reduced rates if she got two friends to rent the other rooms.

"I went to her party. You've never seen anything like it. It was just a little end-of-terrace house, but she had 150 to 200 people there, squashed into all the rooms. There was only one other guy living there – a postman in his 20s. I don't know what he thought. He locked himself in his room. There were police vans circling the road and the house was a wreck. It was a really wild party – the talk of the town for weeks afterwards. My big sister and her husband were really angry because they had to have the whole place recarpeted and redecorated. Their favour to Geri backfired on them!"

GERI: "I really didn't know what I wanted to do. I'd had dreams of becoming famous, but nothing had really fuelled them and they'd gone out of my head. I flitted from one course to the next, got into the acid house scene, then took on a job. I didn't know what I was doing and nothing felt right.

"I went back to college again to do an A-level in English literature after I went for an audition for a part in a political comedy and the director asked me what the last book I'd read was. The part went to someone much better read than me and I thought: 'He's got a point. I'm going back to college.'

"After that I went on a party binge for about six months and then started club dancing at the Astoria, which led me into this career. First I got spotted dancing and got a slot at the Astoria every Saturday night. Then I was picked to dance for a season at BCM in Mallorca, the biggest club in Europe. That's where I did my first glamour shots."

Natalie: "I wasn't bothered when she tried topless modelling. Most of the pictures were tastefully done and she looks really beautiful. There's nothing horrible or dirty about them. My dad wasn't at all shocked – he thought she looked lovely. His first wife was a model and he loved the whole business. I think the only person who might have been a bit upset was my mum. She was a little bit prudish about it, I think."

EMMA: "I was quite nervous when I left home to go to Maidenhead, but I needed to do it if I was going to make a go of the group. My mum was shocked that I went just like that. Sometimes I got homesick. One of the first nights I was there I went in to Geri and said: 'This is my first time away from home and I miss it.' and she was really sympathetic, which bonded us. I went home at weekends and once in the week, maybe. Mum was brilliant, too. She'd drive up and meet me and make me things to eat. I was on social security so I was broke."

PJ: "It was a bit quiet around the house when Emma left home, but she used to ring up and come back a lot. She's around even when she's out, because she's always on the 'phone."

"An early snap. Not quite the international jetset superstars at this stage."

MEL B: "Leaving home didn't scare me because I'd been teaching aerobics in Europe, so I was used to being away.

"I'd been in Austria teaching kids to dance, which had pleased my mum, because I was in a really quiet place where there wasn't any nightlife. But I only taught for an hour a day, which meant I had the rest of my time off, so I found a club on the other side of Austria and went there a few times. When I strolled in at eight in the morning, all the kids would ask, 'Miss, where've you been?' and I'd say, 'Don't you dare tell Mrs Whatever-her-name-is that I've been out and just come in!'

"I did so many different things before the Spice Girls that it's hard to remember what order it all came in. I worked in the Yel Bar as a club dancer, which was fun because I just freaked out all night. I also did *Starlight Express* training for about three months and learnt how to dance on roller-skates, but I missed the final audition."

> **Danielle:** *"When she left home, she went to Blackpool to do a summer season and I went and stayed with her a couple of times. She was living in a house with a few other dancers. It was good because, after her evening show, she taught me to roller-skate."*

VICTORIA: "I left home properly when I was 16 to go to college in Epsom. I went home most weekends, though, because I wasn't that happy there.

"The next year my mum and dad bought me a flat, which was very nice of them.

"The hardest thing about leaving home was actually going back. I really like living at home because I've got a lovely relationship with my mum and dad. Perhaps I don't have quite so much independence as I'd like, but I'm still very happy living at home."

> **Louise:** *"I remember her leaving home to go to performing arts college in Epsom. Then my mum and dad bought her a flat and she lived there with four other girls. I went to visit them with my parents. When you went into her flat there were always ballet tights hanging up and no food in the house. You can imagine it – five girl dancers living together. We started getting on better because she wasn't at home all the time."*

MEL C: "I was a bit scared when I left home and went to college in London, but I was more excited than anything because I was fulfilling my dream and doing what I wanted. It was like a big adventure. I never had any thoughts of returning home and I still haven't. I feel like I know I'm never going home, now. At the time, my dad asked: 'Are you sure you want to do this?' He thought I should get some more qualifications. But my mum always said: 'Do whatever makes you happy.' Eventually my Dad said the same."

> **Paul:** *"Mel loves being alone. I don't know how she stands it, staying in her flat on her own. It's amazing. She's always been independent. My parents didn't try to make her stay on after GCSEs. Our mum's the type who backs us up in whatever we want to do, as long as she thinks it's feasible.*

COLLEGE

MEL B: "I went to the Northern School of Contemporary Dance for about ten months on and off, but got chucked out because I never used to turn up. It's a really good school, especially for people who've never had the chance to learn to dance before, but I already knew most of the technical stuff because I'd been training to be a dancer since I was eight.

"I learnt a lot, but it wasn't challenging enough for me really. And because it was a contemporary school, you had people saying things like, 'I can feel the music through my fingernails,' all the time. I'd say, 'Just shut up and dance,' but no one really got my sense of humour.

"While I was at college, I taught aerobics at the Mandela Centre in Chapeltown, Leeds, twice a week to earn money. I put on my flyers that I wasn't a fully-qualified trainer, but my classes used to be packed out anyway. Loads of men would come, which was funny. I also worked for *Motor Mart Papers* selling advertising space in the evenings for a year before I got a full-time job at *Leeds Weekly News*. For a while I really enjoyed dressing up in little suits and carrying a briefcase, and I was good on the 'phone. But then I got bored."

VICTORIA: "I got a grant at college. All my fees were paid for and for the first year my housing was paid for as well, so I had a bit of money – not much, but a bit. I think you really adapt to how much you earn. I will spend all my wages now, which is loads more than I used to get when I was a student. Amazingly, I probably had more money in my pocket at the end of the week back then. I just spend it all now."

> **Louise:** *"I didn't take her ambitions any more seriously when Victoria went to college. We used to go and see her shows, but she was never the main part.*
>
> *"When she left college, she appeared in Birmingham in* Bertie *– a show with Anita Harris."*
>
> **Christian:** *"I used to go and see Victoria at college and I wondered what she was going to do when she left after three years. She lived in a nice flat there. It was messy, but I think all girls are messy – both my sisters are. I'm definitely the tidiest."*

THE AUDITION

MEL B: "One day I saw an advert for a girl band audition in the *Stage* newspaper, which I bought every week. I thought, 'Let's see what it's about,' but in the meantime I went for a part in *Coronation Street*, which I didn't get. That's probably because my shoe broke as I went into the audition and I had to sellotape it around the heel. They must have taken one look at me and thought, 'Oh no!' At first my mum and I were giggling about it, but I didn't find it funny after a while, and felt really embarrassed.

"I used to go to a lot of auditions, for all kinds of different things. I went up for *Cats* and *Miss Saigon* and reached the last few, but I never got them. It didn't get me down, though. You usually have to sing songs at auditions – something you've learnt and something they give you to do on the spot, to test how you really sing. I'd learnt *The Greatest Love Of All* by Whitney Houston and it sounded fantastic, because I'd rehearsed it for a month. But when I had to sing a song I didn't know, it would always sound appalling.

"I kind of knew I'd got into the girl band, but then I often got the feeling that I'd done really well at auditions."

Danielle: *"Mel taught dancing in Austria and Holland, then did a pantomime in London before she got into the Spice Girls. My mum saw the advert in* The Stage *and told her about it. I remember her going to the audition. I think she wore long socks and a little skirt for it. She really thought she'd got it, so she refused to go to any of the other auditions my mum told her about afterwards. She was really happy when she found out she had actually got it."*

GERI: "I bought *The Stage* every single week. It was my one link to the chances I was looking for.

"I missed the first Spice Girls audition because I'd sunburnt my face skiing, but I'd ripped the advert out of *The Stage* and kept it for some unknown reason. One day I just rang the management out of the blue to ask if they'd filled all the spaces and they told me to come down. So I jumped the queue into the last 12.

"We all had to learn a dance routine which we made up for ourselves. The first six did it, then the second six did it. I was the only one who was picked out of my group. I was told to join the other group, which meant I had to learn another dance routine really quickly. I remember looking at Melanie B and thinking how good she was.

"We also had to sing *Lean On Me* in harmony, and when I was told to sing in a certain key, I thought, 'What?' I was so uneducated in music to begin with, but I've really improved since. Now I even come up with melodies."

Natalie: *"Geri didn't think she was going to get into the Spice Girls because there was so much competition. She had to try doubly hard, and was really lucky to get it because there were so many girls there who were better singers and dancers than her. She definitely won them over because she's so sparkling with loads of personality.*

"To be honest, she's had so many projects that I didn't think we should immediately have a party when she got into the band. I kept calm and waited to see what happened."

MEL C: "I was at an audition for a cruise ship when I noticed someone handing out flyers for a girl band audition. I thought: 'This is it. This is the one.' I got through the first stage, but then had tonsillitis and missed a recall. I got my Mum to ring up and beg them to let me do it again, and they did. For the first audition I wore a lilac knitted little top, some black leggings I borrowed from a friend and my boots. For the recall, I saved up to buy an outfit, and wore long pulled-up black socks, long black lace-up boots which my boyfriend had bought me, a white A-line skirt with buttons up and a tight black t-shirt."

Paul: *"I remember Mel had tonsillitis and couldn't do the original audition for the girl band. So my mum rang up and asked if they would give her another chance. She was lucky. I thought it was a bit of a long shot, but she got in."*

VICTORIA: "I read about the audition in The Stage. When I turned up there were loads and loads of girls there. The only other girl I remember from the first audition was Melanie C. I recognised her from other auditions and thought she always looked really fit. She was very friendly, too.

"At the time, I was in another group that I'd been with for a couple of months. They didn't have a name. Anyway, when I knew that I'd got into the girl band, I told the other group I didn't want to be with them any more. They didn't react very well – they screamed and shouted at me down the phone. It wasn't really a dilemma for me because the girl band seemed a lot more organised. Even the studios used for the auditions were proper studios and it all seemed a lot more professional."

Louise: *"She was always going to auditions for things and I never took much notice. I know she was in another pop group before she was in the Spice Girls, but I don't know much more than that, not even how many people were in it. I know she had to choose between the two bands. My mum helped her over it, but I kept out of it. I never thought the Spice Girls would be the next Take That."*

EMMA: "My singing teacher introduced me to the other Spice Girls. She knew they were looking for someone else and thought I'd be right. I didn't really have an audition. I just did a singing piece for her one day and that was it – I was in. When I was at Sylvia's I loved acting and dancing, but my favourite was singing, which is the hardest

thing to get into. It was easy to go to an acting or dancing audition, but to be a pop star always seemed the hardest thing. So when the Spice Girls came up two years later, I had to do it.

"At first I was on a week's trial, which was a bit weird. I was nervous, but I'm quite determined. I was aware that I shouldn't push myself forward too much at the beginning. But we all wanted the same thing, so I just fitted in."

PJ: *"I don't remember Emma going for an audition for the Spice Girls at all. One day I just found out that she was in a group. I thought: 'Well good luck to her, I hope she does well.' But I never imagined she'd go this far. I never thought she'd be on Top of the Pops. It's a shock."*

"A bit more like it. Once the Spice Girls existed the image came naturally – we just let our individual personalities shine through!"

GETTING TOGETHER

EMMA: "It was quite funny coming into the band late because the others had all known each other for a bit. I had to meet them at a train station the first time and there were quite a few girls hanging around. But as soon as I saw them, I knew who they were. We just clicked straight away."

PJ: *"I thought the other girls were a bit crazy when I first met them. When they came to stay at our house, I saw Melanie Brown naked. I was in my bedroom with the door open and she walked out of the bathroom without any clothes on. I thought she'd be really embarrassed because it was the first time I'd met her, but every time I see her she says, 'You saw me naked!' and laughs. She doesn't get embarrassed about anything.*

"I used to be shy . The Girls would come up shouting 'Hello' and I'd just mumble something back and run into my bedroom. Emma would say: 'This is my brother. Don't worry – he's shy.'

GERI: "At the second audition we had to sing *Signed, Sealed, Delivered* by Stevie Wonder. That was the first time I saw Melanie C and I thought she was really good. She reminded me of Elvis! Melanie B sang *Queen Of The Night* and I thought she was just amazing. Victoria and I sang a bit out of tune, and I'll never forget Victoria saying: 'Look, I may have sung out of tune, but I can do it really.' It was really funny – such a Victoria trait to apologise like that."

Natalie: *"I thought the others were all lovely. I met Melanie Chisholm first of all, then Geri brought her and Victoria round our house one evening when some of my family from Spain were over. The three of them sang for everyone. I met Melanie B after that and thought she was mad. She was incredibly loud, but really funny. I met Emma last and she's just a beautiful little baby."*

MEL B: "I think I saw Vicky at the first audition. I remember seeing Melanie, Vicky and Geri at the second one. As soon as Emma joined us, I thought that everything just came together."

Danielle: *"I first met the other Girls when they all came up to stay here and sang some of their songs. I thought they were all really nice – I think I liked Emma the most, but I got on with all of them."*

MEL C: "Victoria walked in on the day of the first rehearsal and I recognised her from Laines, which was a rival college to mine. Geri walked in and I thought she was a complete nutter, but I really liked her. I thought Melanie Brown was just really cool.

"We all sang *Signed, Sealed, Delivered* one at a time. Because I'd just got over tonsillitis, I was singing a bit throatily, which is why Geri thought I sounded like Elvis."

Paul: *"I first met the Girls down in London when we all went for dinner in a hotel to celebrate signing the contract with 19 Management. I thought they were great and I could see their individual personalities immediately. Geri and Mel B just took over the whole show, as usual."*

VICTORIA: "I was really chuffed when I got through to the next audition. That was the second time I met Geri, who I thought was a complete nutter. I recognised her from the *Tank Girl* audition. She was nicely scatty, with a very friendly nature, so I really liked her. I remember thinking Melanie B was really, really loud but I also thought: 'You are beautiful, absolutely beautiful!'"

Christian: *"When they first came to our home, I was sitting down watching the telly with my mum and dad and Melanie Brown came running in and jumped all over me. She started kissing me and I went bright red. I felt embarrassed then, but now I've got used to it. They're like that with everyone – they like embarrassing people."*

Geri: "Just at the time everything was kicking off I was signing on one week and travelling club class to America the next."

"Here we are celebrating in the offices of 19 Management after signing up with Simon."

MAIDENHEAD

EMMA: When I first moved in with the Girls I had a boyfriend who was a bit of an idiot. I told them about him and they said: 'What are you doing?' They gave me the confidence to ring him up and end it. Not long after that I met another boy. Soon after we started going out, he went on holiday. I was sharing a room with Victoria at the time and every evening I'd be wondering if he was going to ring or not. One night I went to the local disco and when I got back the others were shouting: 'He's rung! He's rung!' I was so happy that I'd been out when he rang. When he rang back I was able to say: 'I've just got in!'

"It was good that I shared a room with Victoria because we were the ones who always wanted to go home. So if we got homesick, she'd drive us both back for the night. Melanie B and I were the most untidy.

"I'd come down in the morning and Mel's stuff would be all over the floor and we'd have our Kormas from the week before still sitting there. Melanie C would always wash up and clear away the rubbish. She'd shout, 'I can't believe you lot!' while we were up in our bedrooms listening to music.

"I was quite a party animal and had a lot of friends I went out with at home. So when I moved into Maidenhead I asked: 'Are we going to go out and party?' We all went out together, but it was mainly Mel B and me. We worked really hard during the day, so sometimes we didn't finish until seven or eight in the evening. Then we'd all make dinner and chill out for the evening. But for us, relaxing was sitting down and writing a song a lot of the time."

PJ: *"I missed Emma, but I knew where she was and I could speak to her if I wanted to. I went up to visit her in Maidenhead with my mum. The girls were living in a nice house. It was tidy, which surprised me, because Emma's not usually tidy. They were all settled in and you could see that they were happy, but I think Emma sometimes wanted to come home. She always gets homesick – she can't be away from her mum for too long."*

GERI: "When the Spice Girls first started out, I didn't really say much about it to my friends and family. They'd been through my past plans and schemes with me and I just thought it would be better to see where it went, although I really did believe in it. I moved straight down to Maidenhead and through myself into it."

Natalie: *"It seemed like ages before anything did happen. The Girls rented a little house in Maidenhead and they all piled in together. It was a nightmare! All of the girls had boyfriends and they were always on the 'phone to them, so it was almost impossible to get through to Geri."*

MEL B: "While we were living in Maidenhead I used to go clubbing every weekend. It was mad. I once woke Geri up at 3am and said: 'Let's go out.' We went to the Ministry of Sound and got back at ten the next morning. Most of the other girls went home for the weekends, and sometimes I did, too. But a lot of the time I'd go out with Geri."

Danielle: *"Still, she rang home every day to talk to my mum. We're both very close to mum.*

"My mum thought Mel was wasting her time at first. She was a really good jazz dancer and teacher and my mum wanted her to be in Miss Saigon. She kept trying to send her to all these auditions, but Mel wouldn't go."

MEL C: "I shared a room in Maidenhead with Melanie B. Originally we shared a big double bed but then we got our own beds. I had Madonna on one wall and Damon from Blur and Oasis on the other. Those were mad times because Melanie and Geri used to argue a lot. They clash when they're living together because they're both really loud. I just stood in the middle with my fingers in my ears. I tried to make it up between them, but I soon gave up because they'd be fighting one minute and best friends the next."

VICTORIA: "When we were living in Maidenhead. I went home most weekends because, even though I loved all the others, I do need to be on my own a lot. But we worked very hard during the week. We all knew what we wanted so we were very

disciplined. Something got us out of bed and working – I don't know what it was."

Louise: "I went up to the house in Maidenhead a few times. I remember the first time I went with my mum and I hadn't met the other girls before. They did us a couple of songs and dances and I was impressed with their voices."

DOING THE ROUNDS: MANAGERS

EMMA: "As soon as I joined the Girls, I could see that they weren't happy with the manager. He was trying to dress us all the same in little dresses and it just didn't feel right. Even then we were sitting down

together to write songs. Geri was great with words, and Mel and I were good with melodies. Anyway, one day we sat down and decided that we could do it our way, even though it would have been so much easier to stay with the management we had. We had someone telling us what to wear and sing, but it wasn't for us. We were full of our own ideas.

"When we went around looking for new managers, we used to burst into their offices and cause a commotion. Mel B was brilliant because she just didn't care. Geri was great because she's so good at talking and gave it all, telling them what we could do. I'd sit there looking cute, Vicky would be looking posh and Mel C would be doing her back flips in the middle of the floor. We didn't have to do a lot, because between the five of us we had something that just slapped people in the face. We went in there being ourselves and put a little *a capella* together, which probably sounded terrible.

"We saw a few managers and went all around the country. We met a lot of people who promised us lots of money and instant success, but we weren't into that. We were looking for someone who wouldn't try and impose their ideas on us. I was a teenager at that time, and if someone turns round to a normal teenager and says, 'I'll give you loads of money and make you brilliant,' you'd think they'd say, 'Yes please', wouldn't you? But for us it was more than just money and singing. It was also about who we were and what we were about.

"We started making demos with some producers because we wanted to go to a manager with a package. We heard through the grapevine that they had a manager who worked for Simon Fuller, so we asked them to put in a good word.

"We'd written a song called *Something Kinda Funny* about how there was something kinda funny going on to bring us all together. Simon heard it and asked to see us. He was the first manager who sat there and asked: 'Right. What do you want to do and how do you want to do it?' He told us how he could help us and take us to the next level, but he didn't try and impose anything on us. We immediately realised that he was the manager we wanted."

GERI: "We were really organised about going to see managers. When we went in, their eyes would always light up. They thought it was great that we had our own songs and you could see they were after a quick buck, but that just did not feel right to us."

> **Natalie:** *"I remember them driving all over the country meeting loads of different people. They were knocking on doors for ages. I wondered if they'd blown their chance. Then they said they'd met this really nice guy called Simon and felt cool with him."*

DOING THE ROUNDS: RECORD COMPANIES

EMMA: "A couple of the girls roller-bladed around the record companies one day, but I was too lazy. I just jogged behind and caught up when one of them fell over! We went to see a few. We wanted a record company which didn't have a lot of pop acts. We wanted to be the centre of attention and have people working hard for us because they hadn't done it before. We also wanted to work in a team and do things completely differently."

GERI: "Before I joined the Spice Girls, I'd made some contacts in the record industry. When I met the other girls, I decided to get some advice from a record company executive. 'Five girl band? It'll never work,' he said. But I felt there was a massive gap in the market. And when someone tells me that something can't be done, that really fires me up."

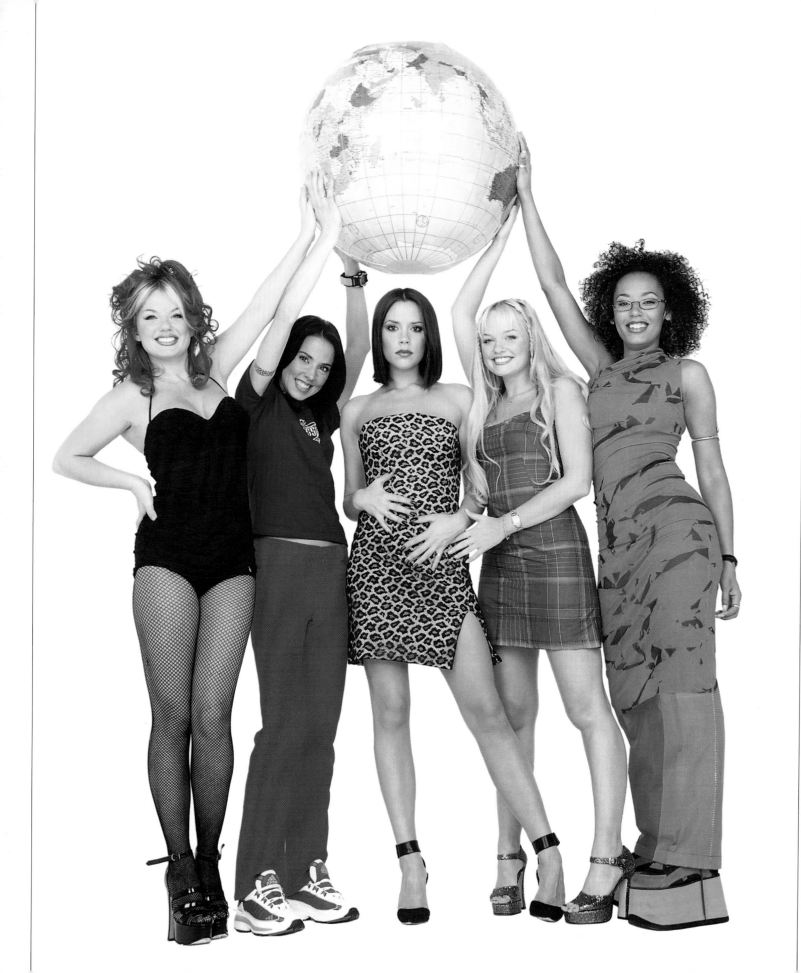

Spice Girls are *GO!*

WE'RE OFF! We had a manager, and were about to sign a major record deal. Next stop, the world!

SIGNING THE DEAL

MEL C: "When I left college we had to write about ourselves and our ambitions. I put that mine was to do *Cats*, but ultimately to get a recording contract. So it was excellent when we signed with Virgin.

When we signed the deal, there was a buffet on the roof of the Virgin offices with loads of champagne. Then Simon (Fuller, our manager) took us to Kensington Place restaurant for a meal, but we were a bit drunk and Victoria had her head in the plate. We had a load of drinks from the Virgin bar and we sprayed each other with bottles of beer in our cab. Simon had to pay the taxi driver to get it cleaned. After the meal we went home and carried on drinking, then had a flower fight, whacking each other with the big bunches of flowers we'd each been given. Victoria just passed out on the spare bed."

> **Paul:** *"I didn't see Mel much when I was doing my GCSEs, but my mum and I picked her up once in London and she stuck some tapes on in the car, saying: 'These are the demos of my new group. You probably won't like them because they're pop songs.' I didn't think much of them because of the bad sound quality. You couldn't hear anything, really."*

MEL B: "It was really exciting to have a record deal. We had been waiting for it for so long, and now, we had the right deals. It was perfect. We did a little performance for everyone. And then we celebrated a bit, before getting a cab to go and meet Simon. Emma spilled a bit of beer on me in the taxi, and then I flicked it back at her and we ended up in this massive beer fight. When we finally stumbled out of the taxi at this really posh restaurant, both we and the cab were absolutely drenched. It was a mess! Simon had to give the driver 60 quid to pay for all the damage. We all sat in this restaurant saturated, with Vicky's make-up running down her face."

EMMA: "When we signed with Virgin, we got all our parents together, because it seemed about time they all met. Obviously, we all knew each other's mums, but we wanted to get them together because it's a bit worrying to see your kids being pop stars all of a sudden. We had a big dinner, which was really nice. It's lovely now, because they all tell each other their worries and we don't have to hear it. It's nice for them to have each other."

> **PJ:** *"I was surprised when she signed a deal with Virgin. It was the first indication that things were taking off, but obviously I didn't realise what it meant, really. At first I thought it meant we'd be getting free Virgin flights and all that."*

GERI: "It felt so good when we got the deal with Virgin. Now all those people who didn't believe a five girl band would work, who had been negative about us, were about to be proved wrong. We all had a really good feeling about the band. It felt right. We were girls tripping out together and sharing such a camaraderie and creativity. We had the same ambitions and all of us were determined to make our dreams come true."

> **Natalie:** *"When they signed to Virgin, they had a party there for all their mums. That was our first celebration, the day we thought: 'Yes, this is really happening.'*
>
> *"When they got the record deal it was like, phew, yes they did know what they were doing. Before that my mum had been getting a bit hysterical, saying: 'Oh no, she's blown it!'*
>
> *"It was a big relief. And when Geri got her first advance it seemed amazing because she'd been skint for so long. She always had six terrible jobs on the go but never had a penny. She was always borrowing money. She didn't buy any clothes or anything. She just went straight out and bought herself a car – a red MG Roadster.*
>
> *"She went from having nothing to going into a garage and shelling out seven or eight grand cash. She's so proud of it. She'll always treasure it. Of course, everyone had a ride in it. No other car could ever have the same sentimental value for her, but it's one of the kind which needs attention, so my brother looks after it now. He's always tinkering with it and making sure it's running well."*

AT THE RACES

GERI: "Virgin had a day out at the races to introduce us to everybody – all the media-type people. We thought it was funny, because it was all stiff upper lip and we were just our normal selves and being really quite mad. Anyway, we jumped on the statue of that old horse, Red Rum. I've got a great photo of us on it, and you can see the security guards in the background running towards us. There were a few journalists there, and I remember we took one into the girls' toilets where the acoustics were good, and then sang *Wannabe, a capella.*"

MEL C: "When we first signed to Virgin, they took us to the races and it was all quite posh and well-to-do, and you know us lot – that makes us behave badly. So we all jumped on top of a statue of that famous racehorse, Red Rum. So, of course, a man came over and shouted at us. I don't remember seeing any of the racing or even betting. I just remember eating and drinking."

"When Virgin signed us they wanted us to burst on to the scene with a bit of a bang. When they threw a big bash for us at Kempton Races, we decided we wouldn't disappoint them!"

SPICING AMERICA

GERI: "Our trip to LA was my first time in America. Originally, I didn't like it. I thought it didn't have any soul – it didn't have any heart. But I think you get used to it. I preferred New York in the sense that it had a little bit more soul to it – an edge. There were more misfits there and anything goes, whereas I felt LA was just full of perfect people. Still, I really like LA now. I also like Miami with all its Hispanic influences. I'm very conscious of the Spanish side of me, I suppose."

MEL B: "I'd never been to the States before. It was a bit scary, actually, because like everyone else I'd heard about the stabbings and shootings and all that. But it was weird. We got out there and this big limo turned up and we thought: 'Oh my God!' It was all a big fairy tale, like being in love and being whisked off your feet. We stayed at a really nice hotel and it was all quite unbelievable.

"I like New York. It's just a little bit more urban – it's more cultural and there are just so many different walks of life. It's definitely cooler than other American cities. There's a more happening scene out there."

VICTORIA: "I had been to America on holiday with my mum and dad, but there were certain parts I had never been to, such as New York and LA. I'd been to Florida, but it was like a real holiday thing, I'd never done any work out there. It was nice to see a different side to it all."

"All the pictures on this page are from our first promotional trip to Los Angeles in November 1995, just a couple of months after signing with Virgin. We flew club class to America and were generally made to feel like stars for the first time – wicked!"

EMMA: "I'd always wanted to go to America, so it was brilliant when the Spice Girls first went. I'd like to go back with my mum and brother, and visit Disneyworld and have a real kiddy day with them. When the three of us are together we're just like kids. We'll never grow out of that. We'll always have a laugh."

MEL C: "I've got family in Canada, so when I was about ten, Paul, my nan, grandad, mum and stepdad went to visit them and then spent a couple of weeks touring around America – Detroit, Cincinnati and Ohio. There was a gospel festival on in Detroit, which was excellent. I loved it, but I knew there was a lot more of the country to see than I had seen.

"When I went back with the Spice Girls, we went to LA. Nowhere's like LA. The next time we went to New York. They're so different and I like them both for different reasons – I can't say which is my favourite. I like the hustle and bustle of New York, but then I like the weather in LA and the over-the-topness of it. At first we hated it because it was really false, but now we've grown to love it."

"Back in LA again in June 1996. We were here to learn kung-fu fighting for the video of *Say You'll Be There*, but there was also a lot of promotional work. *Wannabe* was about to be released in the UK and we wanted to be sure everyone knew our name and what we were about."

WHAT THE FAMILY THOUGHT

MEL B: "My family were really, really pleased once the deal had been signed. We started working and we knew something was really going to happen for us. Finally my mum didn't have to worry about us any more. At last we were going to get our stuff out, get our music heard and have a chance to express ourselves properly to the public."

Danielle: "Mel and I started getting on when she signed with Virgin, but we're still not that close. I think that's because my dad used to say: 'If you two can't get on, then don't talk.' So we stayed out of each other's way. She had her life and I had mine. But we don't argue any more and we're getting closer all the time."

EMMA: "My mum can't go and see one of her friends and say she's really worried about her daughter, because the friend won't know what's going on. But our mums all have us in common. Still, I do have to sit down and tell my mum not to worry every now and then. She's got much better now, because she knows Simon very well. They go out to dinner and he talks to her about it all, which helps."

GERI: "My best friends really are my brother and sister. I have grown very, very close to them. And now I sort of understand my mother and accept her for what she is, and that's it really. When my father died I felt so cheated because I'd just got a really good friendship going with him and begun to identify with the man he was. We shared the same sort of imagination. He was a dreamer and jack of all trades as well. He believed in me and always drove me everywhere. I really was 'daddy's little girl'. When he died, I bottled it all up, but it did affect me later. I wish he could have seen all this."

MEL C: "I kept my parents updated about everything that happened, so they went through it all with me. My mum wasn't ever surprised by any of it. She's the same as me and always thought I could do it. I think my dad was a bit more worried. He asked what I'd do if it all went wrong. I said: 'Well, I'll decide that if it does.'"

VICTORIA: "My family were really proud of me. For absolutely months and months and months, everyone was asking, 'When are you actually going to release something?' because the release date kept being put back, and we were never quite sure whether they were going to release something or not."

"This is from our first holiday together in Maui, Hawaii, back in 1995. When our families saw where we'd been staying they knew we were definitely on to a good thing!"

music week

For Everyone in the Business of Music

2 NOVEMBER 1996   £3.25

We're Number One!

OUR WORLD EXPLODED when *Wannabe* was released in July 1996. It stayed at Number One for seven weeks and suddenly the Spice Girls were big news. Our lives would never be the same again...

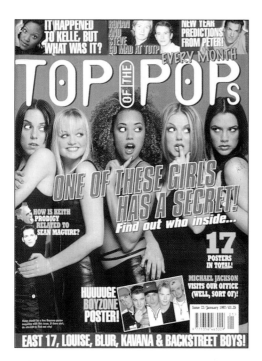

ON TOP OF
THE WORLD

EMMA: "The week before we released *Wannabe*, we were all saying how it would probably go in at Number 41, just out of the charts. But we were still hopeful. We were in Japan when we heard, and although we were away from it all, it was still quite exciting. The five of us sat and had dinner together, which was nice because it was just us. I was ecstatic and couldn't sleep all night.

"One of the first things I did was ring home. I rang my mum and my dad. At first I couldn't get through to my mum. I was trying her mobile and all I could get was: 'The 'phone you are calling is currently unavailable.' In the end I got through to her and she was just screaming!"

PJ: *"It didn't really hit me that Emma was going to do well until she brought out her first song. Everyone was talking about it and then she got to No. 1! I thought: 'Blimey, what's going on?' I didn't suddenly think: 'Omigod, she's famous and everyone's going to love her.' I didn't think of it like that. All my friends were coming up to me and going on about her being famous, but it didn't sink in until recently.*

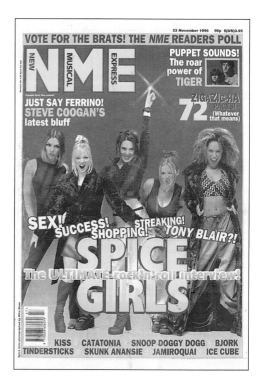

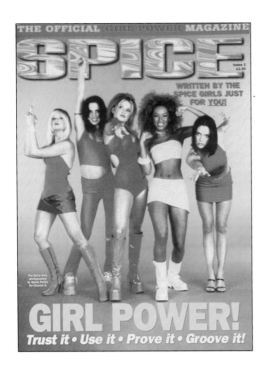

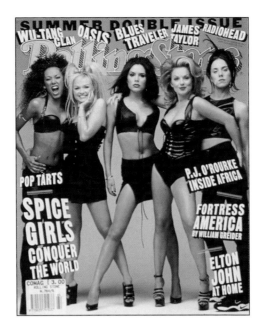

I just took it as it came – she's my sister, she's got a job, she's doing well at it and that's that. Then suddenly I realised she was on telly, in adverts and books and magazines. I was shocked."

GERI: "We were in Japan when we heard *Wannabe* had gone to No. 1. I felt a real sense of triumph because of the cosmic shopping list I'd written six months before.

"To make a cosmic shopping list, you have

to write what you want in the present tense, as though you've already got it. It's about sending out positive vibes to the cosmic universe. Mine said: 'The *Wannabe* video is the best video of the year' and '*Wannabe* is No. 1'

"We'd come up against opposition over releasing it, but we were adamant that this was going to be our first single and I wanted it to be the best video that year. And it was. It was the most played video on *The Box*."

VICTORIA: "My mum and dad used to have parties every Sunday and listen to *The Chart Show*. The day we got to No. 1, I rang them and could hear in the background that they were having a mad party. They were all yelling: 'Congratulations! You're No. 1!' I was in bed in Japan on my own and felt really depressed and cried, because I wanted to be at home with them.

Louise: *"My parents had no idea how big she was going to be. I remember the Girls*

did a concert in Preston and sang Wannabe, *but nobody knew who they were. We went out that night, but nobody recognised them because the song didn't come out till the following Monday."*

Christian: *"When* Wannabe *came out and went to No. 1, I was really proud of Victoria and thought it was brilliant. I couldn't believe it. I thought it was amazing."*

MEL B: "We were in Japan at a restaurant when we heard we'd gone to No. 1. I kissed all the Girls and we all did silly things, like smoking cigars!"

Danielle: *"I was really glad when* Wannabe *went to No. 1. I couldn't believe it. I sat in the garden listening to the charts with my mum and dad and we all ran around when we heard. Then the 'phone never stopped. All the neighbours and friends were ringing, screaming down the line. We had a little get-together that night to celebrate. Melanie phoned and said: 'Can you believe it?' She was swearing, too, and my dad really told her off. He said: 'I don't care if you're at No. 1, you're not allowed to swear!'"*

MEL C: "We were in Japan when we heard we were No. 1. To celebrate we went to the hotel restaurant – just the five of us – and had a big Chinese meal. Then we ended up in the bar with everyone else and smoked cigars and drank champagne. We were overwhelmed. I rang my mum and dad. It was about three in the morning in Japan, and I was shouting: 'We're No. 1!'"

WANNABE

EMMA: "I made all my friends go out and buy our first single. Everyone was asking, 'Get us a single,' and I had to say, 'No. You don't understand. We will not get to No. 1 if you don't go and buy it.' My mum bought about ten the first day it was out. Even now, she buys everything, from the books and magazines to the album. I think all the mums do, even though they get free ones."

GERI: "Wannabe was either a hit or a miss, love or hate. It would either do everything or nothing. We felt, well, if nobody likes it then we have got other songs up our sleeves, but that was the one that we wanted to release.

"We'd already written parts of *Wannabe* when Mel B and Emma came up with the bridge. It was a mad time – we got all excited because we knew we'd found something really good. The video I remember as being very chaotic and cold.

It wasn't very controlled – we didn't want it to be. We wanted the camera to capture the madness of the Spice Girls. I had very big shoes on and fell over a lot. I watched it again recently and thought it was like a comedy. All the other girls gave me the award for being the biggest twit in it! It was definitely the most spontaneous of our videos."

Natalie: *"I didn't think that* Wannabe *was their best record. I said to Geri, 'You've got much better songs. Why are you releasing this one?' She explained that the first release often does nothing, so there's no point wasting your really good songs. She didn't realise that* Wannabe *was going to be a big hit. I was worried that it wasn't No. 1 material. I thought it was a bit too poppy and tacky."*

MEL C: "Wannabe was recorded in under an hour, whereas a lot of the other songs on the album took two or three days at least. The video was a good laugh because it was the first one we made. The day before we shot it, we went to check it out and have a walk through what we were doing, because we knew we were going to do it in one take with a SteadiCam. We rehearsed for a couple of hours, then went back the next day and spent ages getting ready before we started shooting at about nine in the evening. It was really cold and the guy with the SteadiCam looked like Robocop, running around with this weird contraption on him."

Paul: *"In the last year I was at school, I told one of the music teachers that Mel was in a group. I told him all about it and said I thought they were really good. He said: 'Well, don't bet on it. There are a lot of good bands out there who don't make it.' I said, 'I've got a feeling,' but he just laughed at me. When I went back to get my GCSEs the next year, the Spice Girls had released* Wannabe. *For some reason, he wouldn't look me in the eye. I suppose it was because he'd been wrong."*

MEL B: "We were just having a laugh in the studio when we wrote *Wannabe*. It's more of a vibe song than anything else. It had no sit-down planning. The sentiment, the meaning, the lyrics, the rhythm, just happened."

Danielle: *"I didn't think* Wannabe *was that good, but I thought it was a catchy pop tune that could do well. I didn't like it much myself, but I thought it was the type of record that all the little kids would like."*

VICTORIA: "There was a good feeling on the set of the *Wannabe* video, even though it was so cold. It was our first one and I had a shock when I arrived and saw how many people were working on it – all there just for us! It was meant to be a documentation of us, so it didn't have any close-up beauty shots. That made it a bit easier."

SAY YOU'LL BE THERE

MEL B: *"Say You'll Be There* is definitely my favourite single – all the mixes of it are good, even if you can't dance. I like the disco one – that's my kinda groove. I would make a point of going out to buy that, I really would, more so than any of the other tracks. They are all good, but I would seriously think, 'I've gotta have that in my car, now!'

"The song means different things to each of us, but basically it's saying that when you're in a relationship you should be there for each other. You don't have to give them the I-love-you bit, because what's important is being there for each other."

EMMA: "This was one of my favourite videos. We were out in the desert and all getting on really well, so it was a complete laugh. It was very hot and I nearly got sunstroke! Two of the nights, we went back to this hotel in the middle of nowhere – it

was like *Thelma and Louise*. We recorded the song in Elliot Kennedy's studio, which he actually named Spice, after us, because it had never been used before."

GERI: "Every video is really good fun because you get locked into its world for a few days, caught in the time warp of that particular adventure, especially on location. Out in the desert, we really were freedom fighter superheroes!"

MEL C: "We recorded it in our trackies and socks in a studio in the producer's house. It was a cool vibe – dead laid back. A lot of the sentiment in the song has got to do with what we've been through together. We've always been there for each other, so we wrote about that."

VICTORIA: "Geri sings: 'If you put two and two together, you will see what our friendship is for.' I immediately saw the 'two and two is four' pun in that and tried to explain it to the others, but they didn't get it at first. They're no good at maths. It was boiling during the video shoot, and I was in a silly, tight catsuit. I wasn't overkeen on my hair, either."

HONG KONG

GERI: "My biggest performing high came when we did the gig in Planet Hollywood in Hong Kong in October '96. It was so fantastic – we were really happy. Before we went on stage we jumped around to *Do You Wanna Be in My Gang?* on our little stereo. I think our friendship was really balanced and tight at that moment. It was a perfect night. That's also when we realised that there were older people in the crowd enjoying us, which was a good sign."

MEL C: "We had this one night in Hong Kong when we did a showcase of five songs for competition winners and it was just one of those nights – a night to remember. We were all going mad."

I would like to meet the Spice Girls Because they are my Favourite pop group. And I Love their music and singing

Mel. C
Mel. B
Geri
Victoria
Emma

People's Favourites

OUR FANS ARE EVERYTHING TO US.

The Spice Squad has grown and grown
and we couldn't have done it without you...

SPICE: THE ALBUM

MEL C: "When we write a song we have a huge pad and we just write down ideas – even the most ridiculous, silly things. We end up with a big page of phrases and words and put them all together. Every song on *Spice* is about things we've experienced growing up – situations we've been in with friends, with lads and with our parents. Because we've all had different experiences, you get lots of angles on everything."

> **Paul:** *"Mel brought the album home before they'd released anything. I played it and thought: 'That's alright!' Then I played it to my mates. Two weeks before they released the album I said to my mum: 'That's No. 1' And it was."*

GERI: "The thing about the first album for us, is that we'd had the songs on it for a couple of years before the public heard them. Now we're just getting used to the songs for the second album, so of course they seem fresher."

PRESSGANGED

MEL B: "I'm not bothered what the papers say. I don't read them anymore."

EMMA: "I'm not sick of giving interviews, especially when all five of us are there and we have a giggle. I don't like being asked: 'How did it all begin?' because it's a bit of a long story, and when they ask about boys, I just think: 'Hold on a minute. We're about singing and Girl Power.' We've done all this stuff – Cannes, the Brits, a movie and lots of other things – and yet they still want to ask about boys.

"At first it upset me that every boyfriend I've had has sold a story on me. I was with one of them for three years and I never dreamed he'd do that. It was only three or four weeks after we split up, so I suppose he could have been quite bitter at the time. I got a bit down about it, but now I can't be bothered with it. I have to say to myself: 'Come on, Emma! You're having the best time of your life, so don't get upset about the silly little things the papers say.' I've just got to ignore it now. There have been lots of lies printed, but most of them have made me laugh."

GERI: "I think I've become quite blasé about the media. Half the time the papers make up a load of rubbish. Now I don't rush to read them to see if they've written anything about me. There was a lot of pressure when it first started, but I just got over it. You think: 'Oh well, on to the next thing.' Unfortunately, though, my nude pictures haunt me forever.

"I felt quite sad when I counted up four different guys who had sold a story on me. Out of all their stories, there might have

was so un-rock 'n' roll! Although it was a nice story, it always upsets me when someone I know sells a story because it makes me think everyone's got a price."

SMASH HITS AWARDS SHOW

VICTORIA: "The *Smash Hits* awards were great. We were kind of the new ones there, because we hadn't been there before. We won loads of awards, so everyone was paying us a lot of attention. It was one of the first big live things we'd done in Britain. I remember watching the Awards three or four years ago and thinking: 'I wanna do that, I wanna be up there.'

"I remember hearing Mark Owen saying exactly the same thing when Take That appeared on the show. He said he'd watched it a couple of years before and said to himself: 'Yeah, I wanna do that!' It was mad when we were on. My mum and dad were there too, which was really cool."

been about ten per cent truth in them. The funny thing is, the ones I really did have passionate affairs with never sold, which is quite nice. I really appreciate it. I would love to go up to them and say: 'Thanks for not selling out like the rest of them.' It's the ones who don't care about you, who quite obviously didn't have any intimacy with you, who sell. I think they sell themselves out in the end."

MEL C: "We have been in the papers so much, and they have written so much stuff, that it's like water off a duck's back for all of us now. It always has been, because 99 per cent of what they write isn't true. Sometimes they get things a bit wrong, but other times they just make it up from scratch. We don't know where they get it from.

"One guy sold a story on me, and funnily enough I dreamt about him last night. He wasn't a really good friend, but he was an acquaintance. We used to go down the pub together and I would go round his house. Basically, we used to have a laugh, so it was a bit upsetting when he sold some pictures of me, and made up a story."

VICTORIA: "My first best friend was called Emma. She had long blonde hair and blue eyes and I always thought she was really pretty, and I used to go everywhere with her. When we got to secondary school, I wasn't as good friends with her but I still knew her really well. So I'd known her for years, yet she still sold a story on me. It was nothing really bad – a picture of me dressed up as a clown. But I was gutted, mainly because it was at a time when Geri and Mel B had all those sex and rock 'n' roll type stories coming out, and mine was about me being dressed up as a Pierrot at the age of 10. I looked like an idiot and it

ARTISTS: CLOCKWISE FROM TOP LEFT
Claire Fordham
Beccy Mackenzie
Darren Gow

MEL B: "It's basically a love song, but it's got a message – make sure you put a condom on if you're going to have sex. We all think that's very important!"

MEL C: "When we write a song it always reflects the kind of vibe we're on. Sometimes we're not in the mood to write up-tempo jolly party songs and we all sit down to write a nice slow one. So one day we got together and started writing and the lyrics were getting a bit too slushy. We thought: 'Hang on a minute – this isn't right.' So we decided to include a safe sex message – 'Be a little bit wiser, baby. Get it on, get it on.' The video shoot for *2 Become 1* was really tough. It took two days in a studio, which was really cold because there were a load of wind machines going. It was funny because we wanted to get this effect of our hair blowing really slowly in the wind, so we had to lip-synch in double time. It was hilarious singing so fast.

VICTORIA: "I think *2 Become 1* was my favourite video. My coat was wicked in it and it was really different to the other videos – shot entirely in the studio, with high technology and loads of effects. It was really weird having to sing passionately into the camera – I felt a right mug!"

GERI: "The *Smash Hits* awards show was one of our first big performances. We sang *Wannabe* and *Say You'll Be There* and got quite a few awards – our first ones! That was brilliant – I didn't want to get off stage. In fact, at the end everyone had to call me off. I would have been quite comfortable to sit down on the floor in front of thousands of people, cross my legs, and just have a chat with them all."

MEL B: "The *Smash Hits* awards were great. I remember doing a few of the rehearsals and there were lots of different people in the audience watching, who were all really nice to us. It was our first really big performance, although we had sung at a Birmingham roadshow before that."

MEL C: "The British fans have been amazing. The *Smash Hits* poll winners' party was really good fun."

2 BECOME 1

EMMA: "I really enjoyed the video shoot for this. They shot close up on our faces, which was a bit of a strange feeling. It's nice to act – I always look at the camera, think of someone I fancy and give it my all."

GERI: "Every video has a change of vibe, and this was another side to Spice. It was a nice, cosy video. You do get a bit self-conscious singing straight at the camera, but you have to get over that."

viCtora

melc

emma

Girie

melb

VOTE SPICE!

GERI: "I thought that the *Spectator* interview was brilliant. It had both an adverse and a positive effect on us. The positive was fantastic in the sense that it opened us up to a bigger market. Suddenly, the Spice Girls have an opinion on politics! It was comical to think that we could have an effect on the election. Maybe the papers didn't have much else to write about that particular week.

"We are five different girls, with five different backgrounds, so it's just like asking five girls on the street their views. You had one anarchist, one Labour, one total Tory, I was a red, white and blue, and then you had someone who didn't have a clue. That's a real reflection of our society today, which I thought was pretty cool. I don't regret what I said at all. I'm glad I said it."

VICTORIA: "I didn't read that *Spectator* interview. So much rubbish goes in the newspapers, that I don't read any of them. The guy who interviewed us was really conservative and wanted to shape the interview around his beliefs. It's nothing different to anything else we've done – the press always do that. I just think it's a bit ridiculous that at the time of the election the main question to all the MPs was: 'Who's your favourite Spice Girl?' To be honest, I think that one of us lot should have run for Prime Minister, 'cause we could probably have done a better job."

MEL C: "The *Spectator* interview, which had us going on about Margaret Thatcher, upset me quite a lot. Because of where I come from and the way I've been brought up, its a bit of an insult to be thought of as a Tory. But it put us on the front page of the papers for a good week, so we thought: 'Well, any publicity is better than no publicity.'"

Spice Portfolio #2

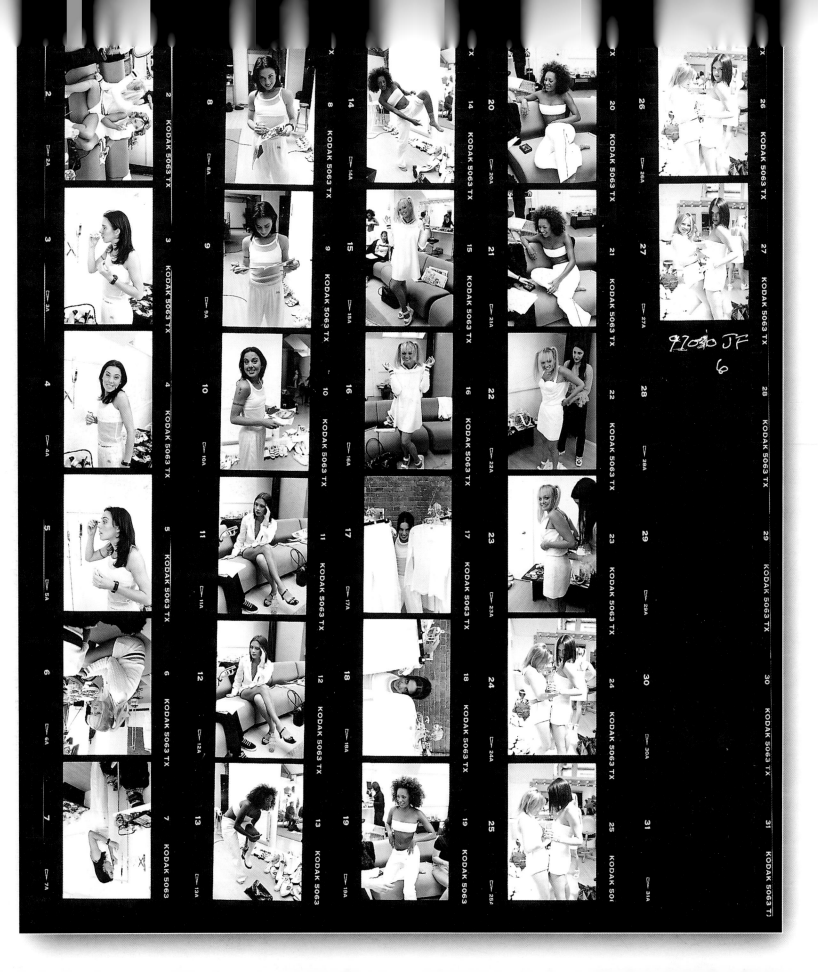

It's a Spice World

BREAKING AMERICA was the next big move.
In Britain, meanwhile, we released our fourth single –
a double A-side – *Mama* and *Who Do You Think You Are...*

CONQUERING AMERICA

GERI: "Everyone wants to make it big in America. It's every band's American Dream, so it's got that extra edge to it. Making it there means a bit more than, say, making it in Taiwan."

VICTORIA: "America is a tough place to crack, but at the end of the day I thought: 'They're no different to anyone else in the world, and we've done well in a lot of other countries.' A lot of bands go out there thinking they've been successful in Britain and all around Europe so they are not prepared to start from scratch with America. But of course the American public had no idea who we were, so we knew we had to start from the beginning and earn respect, and that's what we did."

EMMA: "I really liked America. It's such a huge country and every city is different. Everything's larger than life and very animated. First of all, my favourite city was LA. Now I like New York. I wouldn't live there, though. I'm a London girl."

MEL B: "We treated America like any other country. It has all that cool R&B music, which is kind of scary, because they don't really have pop music out there. But we just gave it our all and it seemed to be alright. We weren't afraid."

MEL C: "All the DJs in America go on about sex all the time. They don't quite

understand us and they say things like, 'So, in *Wannabe*, why do you say: "As big as they are?"' And we say: 'What? When do we say that, then?' And they say: 'You know – "I really really really want as big as they are."' We laugh and laugh. They never get it. We wind them up and tell fibs and stuff. We make up really silly stories and they say: 'Really? Wow!'

"There's a great sports shop in the Beverley Centre in LA called Champs. Niketown in New York is amazing – it's about five floors of Nike. I always buy stuff for my brothers when I'm over there. I try and buy all my family something – Tommy Hilfiger aftershave for my dad, sweatshirts for my stepdad, a nice designer top for my mum, sportswear for my brother and little dinky sports clothes or Disney stuff for my little brothers."

WHO DO YOU THINK YOU ARE

MEL B: "Making the video for *Who Do You Think You Are* was really, really good fun – the best!"

MEL C: "We shot the video for *Who Do You Think You Are* in a really mad club – a real dive. The toilets were horrible and we had to have our make-up done in a Winnebago. The vibe was excellent, though – I think it was my favourite video because it was such good fun. I felt like a proper pop star because we did these individual bits with a guy with a SteadiCam and we had to give it loads as we sang to the camera. It was just how you imagine it when you're young. We were all dressed up, too. I had a dress and shoes on for the first time ever and I felt like Kylie Minogue. It's just a real party video."

EMMA: "The comedians we worked with on the Comic Relief video for *Who Do You Think You Are* were so funny. I had a bit of a nightmare with my clothes, but it worked out in the end. What I wanted to wear all went wrong, so I ended up in a fitted, long dress and I don't usually wear anything like that. I was proved wrong, though, and in the end it did look great."

GERI: "I enjoyed making the Comic Relief *Who Do You Think You Are* video so much. The women were all really warm and funny and nice. The freakiest thing about it was seeing Jennifer Saunders. She looked just

like me and everyone said they thought she *was* me. It was absolutely bizarre – the make-up, everything. It was scary – like, do I really do that? She takes off people and she'd got my mannerisms exactly. It was the most in-yer-face reflection of me, and I was thinking: 'Oh my God!'"

VICTORIA: "The video for *Who Do You Think You Are* was the most fun, because

Dawn French was playing me in it and she was really funny. We had a real laugh. We're going to go out with her one night, actually. She said, 'Come round my house for dinner,' and I said, 'But it'll be all girls, so Lenny can't come.' She said: 'I tell you what, I'll get Lenny to do the cooking.' I said 'Okay' and gave her all our food requirements and we're going to make it a date."

MAMA

MEL C: "*Mama*'s all about how you're such a cow to your mum when you're going through that rebellious teenage stage. Then, when you get a bit older, you realise that whatever she was doing, she was only doing it for your own good. And you think: 'God, I was really horrible.'"

MEL B: "We wrote *Mama* when I was going through a bad phase with my mum. The sentiments are really that your mum's probably the best friend that you've got. Whether she's an over-protective mother or a bit of a landmine, she probably knows you better than you know yourself in some ways.

"My mum was there when we were making the video for *Mama*, and she was really nervous. It was hysterical to see her in such a fluster. That was the day that I decided I wanted my bedroom done out in leopard skin, so I went out and bought loads of leopard skin material in the middle of filming. I've now got a throw, an old fashioned screen, chairs, pictures, rug and lamp – all in leopard skin print!"

EMMA: "It seems really silly, but every time I sing *Mama* I cry. We did it at the Albert Hall for the film and I was looking up at my mum and crying, because it was about us. It was quite an emotional moment.

"I think it will always affect me in that way, especially when I'm abroad. I can't imagine how my mum feels when she listens to it and I'm away."

VICTORIA: "It took such a long time to film the *Mama* video, but it was nice that our mums were there and could see what we're doing. It's good, because they were actually knackered at the end of the day and I said to my mum: 'Ha! Now you know how I feel every day!'"

GERI: "It was nice for our mums to get involved, but for me personally, I found it a bit bizarre bringing my mum to work with me on the *Mama* video. You know: 'This is what I do – come and do it, too.' If you worked in Sainsbury's, you wouldn't get your mum to sit with you on the till. But it was nice for them to get made up, have their hair done and feel glamorous."

Double award-winning girl group say they will never live in the States

HIT PARADE: The Spice Girls led by Geri, right, at the show last night   Pictures: RICHARD YOUNG

Patriotic Spice Girls wannabe Brits for ever

BY DAVID WIGG

THE Spice Girls last night celebrated their double-whammy Brits win by announcing they will never leave England for the United States.

The five singers — who picked up two awards at last night's pop Oscars in London — have sold 2.8 million copies of their debut single and album in America.

Geri Halliwell, sporting a Union Jack mini-dress, revealed: "We owe all our success to Britain and we're proud to be ambassadors of pop for our country.

"Everyone has been amazed at how fast we've hit America, especially us. We've done it even faster than The Beatles.

"Now everyone is expecting us to up sticks and move over there for good, but we'd never do it — we love Britain too much and we're dead proud to be British."

The Union Jack had more trouble supporting Geri — her breasts popped out of her skimpy outfit twice.

"If you will wear a tight dress like this you've got to expect it. Everyone has seen them before so I don't give a damn," she said later. "This is the best night of our lives ever, so I don't care what happens."

The 'girls — Emma Bunton, Melanie Chisholm, Melanie Brown, Victoria Adams and Geri — picked up the Best Single award for Wannabe and Best Video award for their second hit Say You'll Be There.

But while they proved to be the darlings of the public, the industry was less enthusiastic.

Their two successful nominations were decided by public votes — the industry overlooked them when it decided the winners of Best Group and Best International Newcomer.

The show — hosted by Ben Elton at Earl's Court — will be screened tonight on ITV and features the Bee Gees, Diana Ross and The Artist

Formerly Known As Prince. George Michael failed to turn up to collect his award, which was accepted on his behalf by Elton John.

But the event was dominated by the Spice Girls, who kicked it off with a raunchy performance of their new single Who Do You Think They Are?

It could have been aimed at Oasis singer Liam Gallagher, who yesterday claimed he would not attend the show because he'd be too tempted to punch one of the young stars.

Collecting one award Mel C challenged him: "Come and have a go if you think you're hard enough."

A spokesman for The Brits said: "The girls are the big draw this year and they've been brilliant.

Soul star Mark Morrison injected some controversy into the show after last year's antics involving Pulp star Jarvis Cocker.

The singer, in court next month accused of causing criminal damage, was dragged on to the stage by 10 dancers dressed as sexy WPCs.

They then stripped off as he sang his hit Return Of The Mack.

ACTS THAT ARE TOP OF THE POPS FOR 1997

WINNERS: Bee Gees, above last night, were rewarded for years of hits. Gabrielle, left, was Best Female

Best British Male Solo Artist: **George Michael**
Best British Female Solo Artist: **Gabrielle**
Best British Group: **Manic Street Preachers**
Best British Album: **Manic Street Preachers for number one LP Everything Must Go**
Best British Single: **Wannabe by the Spice Girls**
Best British Video: **Spice Girls for Say You'll Be There**
Best British Newcomer: **Kula Shaker**
Best British Producer: **John Leckie (Kula Shaker and Mark Owen)**
Best British Dance Act: **Prodigy**
Best International Male: **Beck**
Best International Female: **Sheryl Crow**
Best International Group: **The Fugees**
Best International Newcomer: **Robert Miles**
Best Soundtrack: **Trainspotting**
Outstanding Contribution: **Bee Gees.**

...and the Winners are...

WE'VE GOT THE BEST JOB IN THE WORLD and winning awards for it is the icing on the cake. Especially when they're voted for by you, the fans...

THE BRIT AWARDS

MEL B: "The Brits were fantastic. The best bit, apart from the actual performance, was being backstage and meeting everyone. We had a really nice conversation with Skin and her band, Skunk Anansie. We flitted about like little school kids, saying: 'Where shall we go now? Shall we go here or over there?' And suddenly it was like, 'Oh right, we've got a performance to do now!'

"There was a big build up too when the lights came on and we were all thinking: 'Oh no!' It was fantastic and I absolutely loved it. The best bit of what we do is the actual performing. When I look back on it I think I could have done it better, but you always criticise yourself, don't you? In fact, it's amazing that us five are up there doing that and looking like that. It's a bit mind-boggling.

"I don't really get nervous before I go on stage – it's more like excitement. You know when you're bursting to do something and you're like, 'Quick! Quick! Quick! Get on with it!' It's a mad rush which explodes when you start to perform. You can lose yourself in it all. I like having a laugh on stage as well – looking at the others, laughing and thinking: 'Ha, everybody, look what we're doing!'"

GERI: "The Brits were such a buzz. It made me feel really proud that we were doing a dance we'd made up in a tiny little beaten-up recording studio in front of all those people and cameras. We had that dance routine almost from the moment we wrote *Who Do You Think You Are* – the very same routine that you saw us doing on the Brits.

"We were all really nervous, but excitedly nervous. I can't describe the feeling when the five of us were standing there with our backs to the audience, knowing that we were going to have to turn around and walk

"Here we are just before the Brit awards. Do we look nervous?"

102

"We did it! Time to let our hair down after the show."

down those steps. It felt like: 'The Spice Girls have arrived!'

"I really miss going market shopping and finding my own little bargains. I don't get to do that any more. Now I draw the look I want and get someone to make it up. That's what happened with the Brits dress. I wanted a Union Jack dress, but our stylist said: 'You can't wear a Union Jack. That's National Front!' I said: 'No it's not. This is the Brits and its perfect.' Just to balance it, I put the peace sign on the back. I drew it, along with the red sparkly dress, and

someone made it. I'm very lucky to have some of the best mediators for my creativity."

MEL C: "Up till now, the Brits have been the highlight of my career. We couldn't believe we were opening the show. When we were facing the back of the stage, we were all screaming! I've never been so nervous. The most nerve-wracking thing was going up to receive the awards because I was worried about tripping over, or stumbling on my words.

"A couple of days earlier Liam Gallagher had said that he wasn't going to the Brit Awards because if he bumped into us, that he would smack us. So I thought: 'I can't let him get away with that.' Noel was there, and he could get the message back to Liam, so I said: 'Come and have a go if you think you're hard enough...'"

VICTORIA: "I have never been so nervous in my life and I will never be that nervous again. I had to be physically put in the car to take me to the Brits show. I was proud – really, really proud. I will never forget Ben Elton saying, 'We have got Sporty, Baby, Posh, Ginger and Scary!,' and I remember thinking: 'Well this is it. I'm going on.' Once on stage, I sort of went on to auto-pilot. It was great, though."

LEFT
"Waiting for the awards to be announced. Nail-biting stuff!"
BELOW
"What a relief!"

THE IVOR NOVELLO AWARDS

MEL C: "Novellos are special because they're for writing, which is something we don't often get recognised for. Most people don't actually believe that we write our songs, even though we do. It was great to get them – they're quite serious awards."

VICTORIA: "It was good to be recognised for not just standing up there and singing, but for actually having a brain and being able to write songs. That was very important. Actually, I remember thinking I wish I had worn a different pair of knickers, because Mel B pulled my skirt up on stage."

GERI: "It was great being recognised for our songwriting. We weren't just being seen as singers and dancers, but as people who could write great songs. But still, making acceptance speeches is so nerve-wracking!"

MEL B: "The Novellos were really good, 'cause we were finally being recognised for writing songs. I wasn't nervous about getting the award itself, because when you're up there it's like follow-the-leader, with your mates."

Lights, camera, Spice!

"It's a wrap! Here we are with all of the people who worked on the film."

MAKING THE MOVIE was excellent fun – the chance to go mad all over London. And our families have supported us all the way...

SPICE: THE MOVIE

MEL B: "Making the film was a major experience and we met a lot of people.

"One day we had to do an assault course and I was really scared because I thought I was going to dislocate my knees. We were supposed to swing over some water on a rope and I hit the water every time. I was so bad at it, but it was quite funny, really.

"Emma, Melanie and I have all done dance, drama and music at school and college, so it wasn't that much of a scary thing to be acting. We found it easy because we're used to it. Even in Maidenhead we all used to act out little scenes in front of each other, so I don't think the film was that difficult. The hardest thing was remembering our lines and where to stand.

"We talked about making a movie three years ago, and then it just happened. But in a way I don't believe it's happening. It won't hit me until I see it on TV or at the cinema.

"My favourite dance film is *The Wiz*, which is a black version of *The Wizard of Oz*. It's fantastic, with Diana Ross and Michael Jackson. I love it."

EMMA: "I hated the early mornings on the set. I'm the kind of person who likes getting up late and going to bed late. Still, it was really exciting to be doing something so different. I think the best scenes were the ones where we're all together, chatting or having a row. It was funny, because they were quite realistic and worked really well.

"Melanie B gets the award for gumbo of the film, because she always got her words wrong! Not really. Sometimes we'd just crack up and wouldn't be able to do a take again because we'd be silly. Then, when we tried to do it again seriously, we'd remember the silly things someone said and crack up again. It would be: 'Oh no! Let's come back to this after lunch!'

"I did a wicked stunt where I had to beat up three male karate experts, throw one of them over my shoulder and another one over my head. I did it all myself!

"The scene we filmed at the Albert Hall was brilliant. Just before we did it we'd been talking about the tour and I was worrying that I might not be fit enough to do it. But that day we were there for six hours doing the dance routines, singing and chatting to the audience without stopping, and I realised that if I could do that, the tour wouldn't be a problem. The adrenalin keeps you going."

MEL C: "My favourite scene in the film is the one we shot in the Albert Hall. It was performing, and that's what we like doing best. We did our new single *Spice Up Your Life*, which is really good, and we were all done up and had mics on like Madonna. All the fans were there, which gave us a taster of what our concerts are going to be like. We all loved it.

"The best thing about doing the film has been the diversity of it. In one scene we might be cracking a few funny jokes, in the next we're all serious and sad, and in another we're performing a song.

"The film's been really hard work, but I've enjoyed it. It's quite sad that it's over, because you get attached to the crew after seeing them every day.

"One of my favourite film kisses is in *One Fine Day* when George Clooney eventually snogs Michelle Pfeiffer. You're dying for them to kiss, so when they do it's really good. My favourite rock 'n' roll film is *Desperately Seeking Susan*, and if I could be any movie star, I'd be Juliette Lewis in *Kalifornia*.

"I never thought I'd be making a film. We always talked about it, but it wasn't really one of my personal dreams. My friends think it's mad.

"When we were on the speedboat down the Thames it was quite scary because Geri nearly fell overboard. She didn't hold on because she never does as she's told! She almost went flying into the river. That was pretty hairy, but exciting, too.

"I always got ready the quickest. It takes me about twenty minutes to get my hair done and twenty minutes for my make-up. I think it's because I like quite a natural look and I don't wear hairpieces in the film like some of the others."

VICTORIA: "I really enjoy acting, so I loved making the film. It was good because the director and the writer gave us a lot of freedom. They understood that we don't like to be dominated. We like to put our own bits in here and there and we want to wear what we want to wear. They tried to put me in a terrible pair of shoes for one scene,

but I just said: 'No way.' Oh, and I got to drive a bus around London, which was well cool."

GERI: "One day on the film set, everyone did this roly-poly thing off the bed for a stunt. I'd done stunts before and I was being really brave about it. Then we all had to jump off something onto a crash mat and do a roly-poly in the air. I kept doing it wrong and landed awkwardly on my neck. It really hurt and in frustration I started to cry. But I did it in the end and I was really pleased that I had.

"There are some fantastic bits in the film. I liked doing the argument scenes and the more intense scenes. I also liked the flash forward to being old bags. It was really good fun dressing up for that scene. I like getting into extreme characters and real moments.

"It was hard work making the film, but when we finished for the day we'd go into a portable studio, and start working on new songs for the second album. *Spice Up Your Life* was written there.

"My favourite screen kiss is in *One Fine Day*. I like the *Rocky Horror Show* and all the old Beatles films. And Elvis, of course. My favourite Elvis film was probably *Blue Hawaii*, when he had to jump off the rocks. I saw all his films. They remind me really clearly of my childhood now and it's nice to get absorbed back into them."

FAME AND THE FAMILY

VICTORIA: "My family have coped with all the fame and stuff really well. I sometimes feel bad that I'm a bit grumpy when I get in from work, but that's because I work hard all the time, and sometimes it's the only place where I can scream and shout. Still, my mum is fantastic. My room has clothes absolutely everywhere, and every day she clears them up for me. My sister is like my best friend, and someone else who has been really good to me is my best friend Maria-Louise. I'd like to give her a big thank you. So there's my mum, my dad, my brother Christian, my sister and my friend Maria-Louise who have all been absolutely fantastic.

"My family have always been supportive of me. My mum's always said to me: 'Stick it out and carry on with it.' A lot of the time she probably wanted me to come home and give it all up, but she made me stick at it and be strong."

Louise: *"It really hits me when I go out with Victoria and everyone recognises her. I wonder how people know who she is. We can't go anywhere now.*

"My friends like it because they like saying they know Victoria, but they're not that impressed. I don't normally tell people that she's my sister. It's not the sort of thing you say, is it? I find it difficult telling people who she is.

"About four months ago I started seeing my new boyfriend and I wondered what he would do when he came round to my house and saw Victoria and David Beckham sitting there. It can be difficult. You never know if people like you for yourself or for her. Luckily my boyfriend's not impressed by things like that.

"My dad loves it. He wanted to make it with his band when he was younger, so he tells people about the Spice Girls all the time. At the beginning, my brother and I both felt a bit annoyed at the way all our parents' friends wanted to know about Victoria all the time, and not us. We didn't get the hump about it, but you're bound to feel a bit left out. Then you think: 'Well I wouldn't want to do it anyway, so I don't care.' I couldn't do what she does. It's such hard work.

"Our relationship has got better and better. We've both grown up – she's had to grow up quickly, all of a sudden. Obviously, she needs someone to talk to and I do, too – and I'm probably one of the only people she can trust. We talk as much as we can. Before she was with David, we used to go out quite a

lot together in the evenings and at weekends, but we can't go to clubs now.

"Sometimes there's a bit of tension when Victoria gets home from work really late and she's tired. Apart from that, it's still a happy house. It's always noisy, with people popping in and out."

Christian: "My dad's always talking about her and showing off the gold discs we've got. My mum doesn't talk about it so much. She's used to it now. I said to her that I thought it was unfair to talk about Victoria all the time, and not myself and Louise. So she doesn't anymore.

"Things are just the same as before. We still go out for meals together. I do get people I haven't seen for years coming up and wanting to talk because my sister's a Spice Girl, but apart from that, life's pretty much the same.

"I wouldn't like to do what Victoria's doing. She's hardly ever home – getting up really early and coming home late at night. I just don't think I'd be able to cope like she does."

MEL B: "I think my dad sometimes gets a bit shocked by how famous I am, but of course he still sees me in the same way. My mum and dad still live in the same house. They will not move, no matter how much I want them to. You can see into their front window, which I don't like when I go home. The whole street knows I'm there, and all they have to do is walk past the house to see what we're all doing. But they've lived there for years and they think: 'Why should we have to move?'"

Danielle: "It wasn't that bad at first, but I'm a bit sick of people going on and on about it. My friends want to know all the gossip and they ask me to get autographs for them. I spend a lot of time with Melanie's friend Charlotte, because I know she's not going to go on about it. It's amazing how people change. Some of the friends I've had for years have totally changed – there have been a lot of jealous people. I suppose it's good in a way, because you get to know who your real friends are."

EMMA: "I still go shopping to high street shops with my mum or a security man. I get fans coming up, obviously, but I just sign autographs and that's it. It's a bit harder to do it now, but I just stick on a cap and a trackie and keep my head down. I'm a big fan of Top Shop and I couldn't bear not to go in there.

"I never get lonely because there are always people around. I think of myself as lucky. My mum's got lots of friends, but probably only a couple of true friends, whereas I've got four, as well as my mum and Simon. So that's six! We all have arguments, but we'll always love each other, like sisters."

PJ: *"We're really close now. I think it's because we've got older and can understand each other more. I know that when Emma comes home from work she's tired and just wants to relax. And if I want to do something, she doesn't get in my way, either.*

"Still, I often go and lie at the end of her bed and have a chat about what we've been doing, or watch a film.

"They call Emma Baby Spice. I'd call her Bad Baby Bunting, because she can be naughty when she wants to be, but she'll always get away with it. That has annoyed me sometimes. For instance, if I've got a bag of crisps and she wants them, she'll get them. Mum will say: 'Go on, give them to her. She's been working all day.' Work's been her excuse for a while, but she should be used to it by now. Still, she's always been able to get away with more than me because she's the girl, the soft one, and I'm the boy who has to take all the rough stuff. I don't mind, though. Sometimes I ask her to ask my mum to get me something, because she can do it. She's good at that.

"I've really learnt from Emma to stick at whatever you want to do, no matter what anyone else says. That's what she's done, despite what all the papers have printed and what other people have said. She's still going for it and she's doing well. I'm pleased for her and I admire her for it."

GERI: "When we were writing *Mama*, I wasn't getting on well with my mother, but now I do. Maybe we all expect too much from our parents. We see them as perfect individuals when we are children and then when we grow up we sadly see things more clearly. We see their imperfections and feel disappointed. I was going through that stage then, and I am coming out of it now. In the song, it goes: 'But now I see through your eyes why you were misunderstood.' As you grow older you do see your parents' point of view – that they were only trying to do what was best for you.

"I now realise the value of family. What's brilliant about having a sister is when, for example, it's a weekend and your other friends have let you down, you know you can always go out with your sister. I would say my sister Natalie is my best friend.

"I feel so lucky. I've also got a good relationship with my other sister, Karen, and I'm a lot closer to my brother, Max, than I've ever been before. He's a really good friend, now."

Natalie: *"Geri's success has definitely affected our relationship. We get loads of strangers intruding on our life. In some ways it ruins our friendship, because it stops us doing all the things we're used to doing together. We can't go to Pizza Express or the cinema or for a drink together anymore. We used to spend all day at Camden Market, but we can't do that now, either. I find it a bit of a pain. Although I'm happy for Geri that she's famous, I sort of preferred it when she wasn't.*

"I worry about how much pressure there is on the Girls to be fantastic all the time. Everyone's looking at them. I hope Geri's coping okay. Still, as long as she's got friends and family to pour her heart out to when she's feeling tired and low, then it's going to be okay. She knows that we're all there for her. She can turn up at my mum's, my brother's or my house, lie in the corner and we'll look after her. We'll put a blanket on her, get her something to drink and tuck her up. It's not all glamour!"

LEFT
"Lounging in our technicolour dressing gowns."
RIGHT
"Bye! Heading home in the Spice bus."

MEL C: "My mum has always supported me in what I want to do. She's in a band, so she knew what could happen if everything took off. I don't think it's had much effect on my family, really. We still sit around the telly, and watch the football when I go home."

Paul: *"I had a lot of friends before the Spice Girls took off, because I'm one of those people who will have a laugh with anybody. I used to take people at face value, but now I'm seeing who my real friends are. I've been let down a few times, but I'm a good judge of character, so it doesn't bother me. I know who's using me and who's not, and I don't have anything to do with the ones who are.*

"I'm quite close to PJ, Emma's brother. We always go out together when I'm down in London. I really like him. He's the kind of person who will do anything for you and he knows some really nice people."

Spice Portfolio

#3

Rich and Famous

IT'S TOUGH AT THE TOP but we wouldn't change a thing. And just because we're famous doesn't mean we've forgotten who we are…

RICH...

MEL C: "Having money's really nice because it means that I can help my family out. I love buying presents for them. My mum's done so much for me, I want her to share in what I've got."

    Paul: *"One day last year, my mum told me I could go to Halfords and pick out a bike for Christmas. I chose one for about £100 because I thought it would be out of order to go any higher than that. Then Mum asked if I liked another one, which was about £400. I said, 'Yes, it's alright, isn't it?' and laughed. She said: 'Then we'll get that one for you. Mel's paying for it.'*

I wouldn't have it at first, but then they brought it out and I just went green. I was out every day on it. That was the day I realised she was going to be famous, because she finally had some money. She spent most of her first advance on her family."

VICTORIA: "It's really nice when you can give things to your family and buy them nice presents. My family never take the mickey, and they never ask me for anything, but I always treat them to things. I got my brother and sister a convertible VW Golf car each as a surprise. I went to the garage with them and said: 'Here are the keys. You can drive them at 12 o'clock.' They were over the moon about that, so it

was really cool. Just giving other people things and being able to put a smile on people's faces is fantastic."

EMMA: "I have never been a money person. I've always been spoilt with love, and I haven't been brought up with money, so it doesn't affect me at all. Even now, if I was doing this for nothing, I would still be doing it. I really wouldn't be bothered if I had no money, I would still live in the same way. The only difference is, I've got a flashier car and a bigger house, but I've still got the same people around me.

  "What is good now, is that I can help my family out and give them things they've always wished for. At the moment I'm buying a house and it'll be so great to see my brother and my mum in the garden, because we've never had one. My brother's always been into drumming but he's never been able to afford a drum kit, so hopefully I'll be able to get him one and he can pursue his dreams. Eventually he wants to be a fireman, but there's a five year waiting list at the moment.

"I'm still a bargain-hunter. I went to Prada (very expensive posh frock shop) with Vicki the other day, and I said: 'Hey! I've seen that in Top Shop for £15.' It seems like all designer clothes are black, and the shoes have pointed heels. They look like granny clothes to me, but Victoria looks beautiful in them."

GERI: "Suddenly, having money and fame, everything's so much more accessible. At the same time, I find it sad. All the things I have are great and I can get everything free now, but I could have really done with those things when I didn't have any money! That's the way it goes, I suppose. One thing that frightens me is that I get a lot of things done for me and I worry that I might lose my sense of independence.

"I always think I mustn't carry too much, but then I buy a lot of tacky trash in places like Acapulco airport. Since I've had some money I've filled up half the playroom in my house with toys. In America everyone else seems to spend their money on clothes while I go into FA Schwartz and spend about $500 on toys – cuddly toys, Buzz Lightyear, everything."

MEL B: "Being rich hasn't changed me because I used to spend money as though I had lots of it, anyway. I've always bought clothes until they come out of my ears, so that hasn't changed. Now I have money, I just spend it in the same way. The difference is that I've actually got it to spend and I can do more for my family financially."

...AND FAMOUS

GERI: "Fame has changed me a little bit. I'm still hyper-hyper-hyper and enthusiastic, but I've mellowed a bit. Maybe it's because I've gotten older, though. Your horizons broaden and grow when you experience different cultures. I would like to think I'm very grounded. Death keeps me grounded. I remember the hardcore reality of life when I need to step back and think about what really matters.

"I feel comfortable now, but I still have that drive, that little nagging thing, a burning restlessness inside. I've always had a mad imagination and loads of ideas and I really appreciate the way everyone is letting me exercise them. What's great is that the Spice Girls are more than a band – there's the magazine, the book and the film, too.

"I like the vocality of fame. It gives you more freedom of speech and a louder voice. I have to plan my life more carefully now, though. I think a little bit more about the consequences of my actions. I'm a bit more wary of people, although I don't want to become hardened to the world. I still want to be open to people as well. But if you have an open heart, you have to have an open mind with it.

"I've really noticed how much I've started to talk to myself – openly and loudly – when I am alone. The other day I was walking in a field by my cottage and really nattering away to myself – giving myself a good talking to, basically. You see I've got all the philosophy and ideas on how to get on in the world – be a good person and get through it – but sometimes applying that to my real true self is a different matter. So I'm almost like two people, and one has to speak to the other one. If I'm a bit down in the dumps, its: 'Come on girl, get a grip!'

"I think lots of things happen for a reason. Recently I had a power cut and couldn't go on my running machine or use my computer. Therefore I had to stop and do nothing, which I took as a sign that I was meant to have a rest."

Natalie: *"Geri always wanted to be famous and she didn't care how. Everyone knew it. I didn't think her career would be in singing. I thought she'd be a TV presenter or something, because she used to go for TV castings and did a short course on how to be a presenter. I wasn't 100 per cent sure she'd make it because I know how competitive that world is. I knew she'd be able to do small things, but I didn't guess she would be mega-famous. I always hoped she would, because I knew she'd be really miserable if it didn't happen. She wanted it so much that I knew she'd be unhappy for the rest of her life if she didn't make it.*

I'm not completely surprised at how famous she is, though. It's not like she was a quiet child who suddenly became a pop star. It's no big shock, but I'm still amazed by her worldwide success. When I see her on telly I think: 'That's not really my little sister. That's somebody else.'"

MEL C: *"I've always wanted to be famous and I love it. It's great that everyone knows who you are and wants to take photos of you. I feel more comfortable being famous and I'm more at ease with myself now than I've ever been. I was always striving for something before, and now I feel like I've got it. There are a lot of restrictions on my life, but I don't mind. I have and would sacrifice almost anything for this.*

"I've become a lot more of a loner since it all happened. I always used to have people around me, but now I enjoy being on my own. Going home is nice, getting away from everything. I never get lonely. In fact, I wish I had more time to feel lonely. I'm lucky, because no-one disturbs me there. Fans knock on the door of my Mum's house, but not my flat in London."

Paul: *"When Mel comes home now, we don't speak about the Spice Girls. We discuss things we'd talk about anyway, even if she wasn't in the band. When she's back, the last thing Mel wants is for someone to go on about the Spice*

OPPOSITE PAGE
"Girls just wanna have fun!"
LEFT
"Loud and proud! Geri and Mel B giving it some."

Girls. That's her work. She doesn't ask me about my job, so why should I ask about hers? We just have a laugh. We go out in the car with the windows open and the music blasting. When she's with me, she likes to do the things she can't do in London. Sometimes she finds it a bit hard to unwind, but mostly she's fine.

"I hate bigheads so I said to our Mel: 'If you ever get a big head with all this stuff you're doing, don't bother speaking to me.' But she hasn't. I think her head's smaller, to be honest. I don't know how she copes with it all, though."

MEL B: "I think fame can change people because you can get paranoid when a lot of people are watching everything you do. I've learnt a lot from it, so obviously I will have changed, but it's hopefully all for the best. I've grown up a bit and seen a lot of things.

"If I'm going out, I have to tell somebody where I'm going in case anything happens, which is a bit like reporting back to your mum. That's okay. My mum's not in London, so having people looking out for me makes me feel quite safe.

"I drove my Alfa (smart Italian convertible) to the gym the other day. I had the roof down and this guy said something very rude to me like: 'I want to get you.' I said, 'Oh yeah? Well we'll see about that,'

and started to drive off. But I was stuck in traffic, so I just had to put my glasses on and turn the music up loud! Then I thought: 'Hold on a minute, he could just reach over and grab me!' That sort of thing is sometimes a bit scary, but I think if you can't look after yourself, who can?"

EMMA: "I've got responsibilities now I'm famous. I've always had friends and I used to go to the pub and meet them all the time, but I can't really do that now, because there are always people around that you can't fully trust. But I enjoy what I'm doing so much that I think there'll be plenty of time to go to the pub later on.

"The other Girls help me keep my feet on the ground. And my mum does, too. When I get home she'll say: 'Your room's a mess! What do you want for dinner?' I go to my bedroom whenever I want a quiet moment.

"Now I'm famous, I don't suddenly think I'm great. I just want to put a smile on someone's face, like so many other people do. When you go into hospital, the nurse always makes you laugh. I want to do that, too."

PJ: *"It's good for Emma to be in the position she is, but I don't know if I'd like it myself. She's used to it because she's been acting all her life. Luckily, my friends just treat her like my sister, not a Spice Girl.*

"When it all first happened they said:

'Don't worry, Paul. We're not going to start asking you to get us loads of autographs or anything.' They know she's famous and they like it because they know her, but it doesn't bother them. None of them have changed because of it."

VICTORIA: "When I was really young my mum dragged me to see a Barry Manilow concert at Wembley and when he did *One Voice* everyone held up their lighters and sang along. I sat there, looking at the stage, thinking: 'I want to be up there.' I had a real flashback to that moment the other day when I heard the ad for our concerts on the radio. Hearing 'Spice Girls: World Tour' freaked me out quite a lot.

"I used to dream that when I went shopping there would be books and pencils and pencil sharpeners with my name on – I imagined things like that all the time. Now it's actually happened, which is quite strange.

"The best thing about being famous is being able to get up on stage. That is absolutely fantastic and you can't beat it. Another thing I enjoy is seeing my mum and dad proud of me."

Danielle: *"I don't think Victoria knows how famous she is. She still thinks she can go to Tesco on a Saturday afternoon and do some shopping. Even now, when I see her on the telly, I don't think it's Victoria. When I hear Spice Girls on the radio I don't think, that's my sister. I've got my sister and I've got a Spice Girl. They're two different things.*

"I never thought this would happen to Victoria. When I was younger I used to look up to people like Bros and I never thought my sister could be bigger than them. I still don't realise how big she is. It's quite hard to adjust."

Christian: *"I never thought she would be where she is today, but I thought she would do well in life through her dancing. She was good at what she did and I thought she'd get into some big show. She always wanted to do well."*

SPICE UP YOUR LIFE

1st Verse

WHEN YOU'RE FEELING SAD + LOW
WE WILL TAKE YOU WHERE YOU WANT TO GO
SMILING, DANCIN' EVERYTHING IS FREE
ALL YOU NEED IS POSITIVITY.

Into the Future

WE LIVE FOR THE MOMENT but people are always asking what we're going to do next. Well, we've been in the studio and now we can't wait for you to hear the new album…

THE NEW ALBUM

GERI: "The new album is a reflection of what we've seen and all our experiences. So it's very up-to-date. We demoed about thirty songs originally, and then chose the best ones. Some of them were written on the set of the film – *Too Much*, for instance. Going into the studio was a great way of winding down after filming."

MEL B: "The new album is going to be different to the first one. It's just as full of good, strong, positive things, but making it has been more relaxed this time. I think the singing and lyrics are better this time."

MEL C: "*Spice Up Your Life* is probably my favourite song on the new album so far. I think it's the next *Wannabe*. We always wanted to do a carnival tune and write a song for the world, after all our travelling. What could be better than *Spice Up Your Life*? We wrote it in a day.

"At the moment I'm having a bit of a love affair with the second album and I like it even more than the first. Maybe that's because it's fresh and new and it's gone so well. I think it's going to be called *Spice World*. We haven't had the luxury of lots of time that we had with the first, when if we weren't feeling inspired we just went home. Now we're on a tight schedule, but luckily it's all come together and gone alright."

EMMA: "One of my favourite things is actually writing songs and singing in the studio. I love that feeling of getting behind the mic and making a song. I'd done some singing for TV adverts in the past, so I'd been in the studio before, but it was very exciting doing it for the first time with the band. It's just you and a mic and you're live. When I sing I always shut my eyes to get into the mood and feeling of the song.

"*Spice Up Your Life* is probably one of my favourite new songs, because I like dancing to it. Its a real 'shake your thang!' number, and kids love it. The response we got when we did it for the film at the Royal Albert Hall was amazing. The whole crowd was dancing and had all the moves, and they were singing along! I hope its going to be a hit."

VICTORIA: "I think that the tracks we have recorded for the new LP are a lot more mature. It was a bit nerve-wracking to begin with, because the first album went so well. There is a lot of pressure to do better. But we all surprised ourselves in the studio, and are proud of each other. We really knuckled down and put together some brilliant tracks."

Saturday.

You're not alone
no you're not on my mind
you were the victim of your crime
I left you behind
Oh, you were a fool
to treat me that way
I'm not gonna let you
I'm gonna forget you
there's nothin to say.

THE FUTURE

MEL C: "Ideally I'd like the Spice Girls to go on forever but I don't know if they will. Obviously we're really popular at the moment, but it all depends on what people want in the future. I know we all want to have kids and families, so maybe we'll take some time off for that as well. But I want to be famous forever and die a legend.

"I'd like to have children by the time I'm 35 – either two or four. I don't know what I'd call them – something unusual and not traditional, but nothing as stupid as Paula Yates's children's names."

EMMA: "We're really looking forward to the tour coming up. It's going to be a great show – we're gonna try all different dances, some salsa and a bit of Spanish and hip hop. I always have a lump in my throat when I go on stage, I get this rush of excitement.

"Of course, I'm going to be away from home for a long time, and at first I thought: 'It's gonna kill me', but I'm getting used to the idea. My mum's going to come out as much as she can. Still, I've got four of my best mates around me, and I know I can rely on them. Plus, I'm going to see the whole world in a year."

GERI: "I can't wait to do the tour. Being on stage is the biggest high you can get. It'll probably be like a travelling circus!

"I was thinking the other day that my future lies in my imagination. The Spice Girls will always be the Spice Girls and I will always be a Spice Girl but I am sure it is inevitable that we will all progress and do other things, eventually. I know we will. That's natural, that's evolution.

"I have been running since the day I left home, trying to get far. I haven't arrived yet, but you have to enjoy every moment of your journey on the way, because it's just as good as reaching that point of achievement."

ABOVE
"Mel C relaxes between takes."
BELOW
"Mel C and Victoria get a helping hand from Biff."

OPPOSITE PAGE: LEFT
"Sofa, so good!"
RIGHT
"Come and have a go if you think you're hard enough!"

MEL B: "I think I'll always work, whether it be in music, dance, film, drama or whatever. Whether or not I'm famous I always want to give something back to people – maybe by doing charity stuff, or speaking up for what I believe in. But at the moment I live from day to day. I'd like to settle down and have children some time, but I'll never stop working."

VICTORIA: "I am really really looking forward to the tour, which is probably going to be the highlight of our career so far. Getting up there and performing to the fans who have put you up there is the best thing ever."

VIVA FOREVER
I'LL BE WAITING
EVERLASTING, LIKE THE SUN
LIVE FOREVER
FOR THE MOMENT
EVER SEARCHING FOR THE ONE.

See ya later...

MEL B: "My message to you all is, RAAA! Not argh! RAAA! Like a tiger."

EMMA: "I hope you're being positive, and having lots of fun and I can't wait to see you on tour. Wherever you are, stay cool and spicy."

VICTORIA: "A big, big thank you to all of you. Without you, we're nothing. We get a lot of positive messages in our fan mail, and that makes it all worthwhile. So keep strong."

MEL C: "I'd like to say a massive thank you to our fans for always being there and supporting us in the way that you have. Just stick with us, because we've got loads more for you. And enjoy the movie!"

GERI: "My advice to any fan is never lose that child within. Walk away from negativity. If anybody is negative towards you, and you have to put up with it, see it as a challenge and a test of your character. Life is a lesson. As long as you are a good person and you have integrity, you will always get what you deserve."

A Brief History of Spice

EMMA BUNTON

born 21 January 1976 ~ also known as: **Baby Spice**

Emma's showbiz career starts early when she becomes a child model. Attends St Theresa's School, London, then the Sylvia Young Stage School, which she is forced to leave at 14 for financial reasons, only to return three weeks later on a scholarship. After school, she studies drama at Barnet College for two years, then joins the London audition circuit in search of work. She is given a few very small TV and advertising roles.

GERI HALLIWELL

born 6 August 1972 ~ also known as: **Ginger Spice**

Begins her education in Spain before moving to London. Attends Watford Grammar School for Girls until 1988, then moves to Cassio College where she studies tourism and travel for a year and later she passes her A-level English. In 1991 she is spotted in a London club and whisked off to Majorca as a club dancer for six months. Other jobs include: TV presenter, Turkish gameshow hostess, glamour model, cleaner, barmaid, shop assistant and aerobics teacher. Shares stolen bag of popcorn with Victoria at the *Tank Girl* auditions.

MELANIE BROWN

born 29 May 1975 ~ also known as: **Mel B** ~ **Scary Spice**

Attends Questfield Primary School, then Intake High School, Bramley, Leeds, where she is one of 30 pupils selected every year for special training in dance, drama and music. Leaves school at 16, dances in various shows in Blackpool, gets sacked from a pantomime in London, teaches dance around Europe, gives aerobics classes in Chapeltown, Leeds, wins Leeds Weekly News beauty contest, sells advertising space for newspapers, entertains the armed forces in the Gulf, Germany and Northern Ireland and sporadically attends the Northern School of Contemporary Dance. Constantly travelling between Leeds and London to attend auditions.

MELANIE CHISHOLM

born 12 January 1974 ~ also known as: **Mel C** ~ **Sporty Spice**

Begins school at Southgates Infant School, Runcorn, moves to Brookvale Junior School and then Fairfield Junior School, Widnes. Attends dancing classes two evenings a week and all day Saturday, every week. After five years at Fairfield County High School, she accepts a place at the Doreen Bird Performing Arts College, Kent, where she spends the next three years. Bumps into Melanie Brown and Victoria at auditions in London.

VICTORIA ADAMS

born 17 April 1974 ~ also known as: **Posh Spice**

Attends Goff's Oak Infants, Junior and Middle Schools, followed by St Mary's High School in Cheshunt, Herts. Attempts a Saturday job in a wedding shop, but is soon offered alternative employment on the catwalk. Leaves home to study at Laine Arts Theatre College in Epsom, Surrey, for three years. Returns home and starts auditioning for London shows.

Late 1992

Geri, Mel C, Victoria, Emma and Mel B meet on the auditions circuit while chasing work in adverts and shows, and as TV extras.

March 1993

Mel C, Victoria and Mel B meet again at an audition for an all-girl band, which was originally advertised on flyers and in *The Stage*: "R U 18-23 With the ability to sing/dance? R U streetwise, ambitious, outgoing and determined?" Each girl is given a 30-second slot to prove themselves. Geri misses the first audition, but wangles her way into the final recall and is chosen to form the group along with Mel B, Mel C, Victoria and a fifth girl, Michelle Stephenson.

June 1993

The five girls spend a trial week in a recording studio. The others notice that Michelle lacks the commitment they share.

July 1993

Michelle leaves the band and Emma Bunton joins.

July 1993 – March 1994

The Spice Girls live in a house in Maidenhead, rehearsing dance routines, going to the studio and eating a lot of toast.

August 1993

Geri comes up with the name Spice during an aerobics class. It seems to fit "because we're all really different", says Emma. And they've already recorded a song called *Sugar and Spice*.

October 1993

They take control of their destiny and create their own Spicy movement after a successful showcase performance to producers in Maidenhead. On the same day they leave their managers, Mel B and Geri keep the drive going by tracking down writer Eliot Kennedy in Sheffield in the middle of the night and persuading him to work with the Spice Girls.

October 1994

With a catalogue of songs, demos and dance routines, the girls set out to find the right manager. Travelling around in Geri's car with a filofax and a 'phone, they go to numerous meetings around the country. A PR man, Mark Fox, introduces them to Absolute, who go on to produce their first album. Through Absolute they hear about Simon Fuller, Annie Lennox's manager, and finally meet him a few weeks later.

March 1995

The girls sign a management deal with Simon.

Spring 1995

They go into the studio to lay down masters of the songs on *Spice*.

March to August 1995

Several record companies battle it out to sign *Spice* while the girls try to decide which one is best for them. Virgin Records throws a surprise party for them before they fly off to explore record deals in LA – club class.

September 1995

The Spice Girls sign with Virgin Records, which seems to be the company most sympathetic to their needs. The Girls pay back their first management company for its investment during the early days of their career.

October 1995

The Spice Girls perform *Wannabe* to a journalist in the ladies' loos at Kempton races and climb all over a statue of Red Rum. Angry stewards fail in their attempts to restrain them.

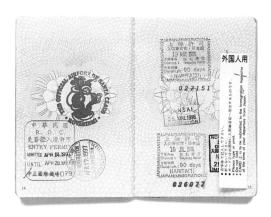

November 1995

The Girls sign with music publishers Windswept Pacific, then head to LA for a promotional tour.

September 1995 to July 1996

They continue to write songs, record and work on dance routines.

April 1996

They shoot their first video, for *Wannabe*, at St Pancras station in London.

May 1996

The *Wannabe* video gets a trial airing on *The Box* cable pop channel. It's a smash hit and is played 70 times a week. Their first music press interview appears in *Music Week*. In LA, they learn how to kickbox for their next video.

8 July 1996

Wannabe, their first single, is released and goes in at No. 3. The Spice Girls are the first British group to top the charts with their debut single. *Wannabe* stays at No. 1 for seven weeks and sells 1.25 million copies in the UK alone. *Wannabe* goes on to be No. 1 in 31 countries.

18 July 1996

Their first national newspaper interview appears in the *Daily Star*.

September 1996

Their second video, for *Say You'll Be There*, is filmed in the Mojave Desert before they fly to Hong Kong.

14 October 1996

Say You'll Be There is released and goes straight to No.1.

November 4 1996

Their debut album, *Spice*, is released, and is awarded a silver disc on advance orders (60,000). Two million copies are sold in two weeks.

November 25 1996

A late-night cable channel offers each girl £1million to strip! They refuse.

December 1996

The Spice Girls win three trophies at the *Smash Hits* awards at the London Arena, including best video for *Say You'll Be There*.

12 December 1996

Interviewed for the *Spectator* magazine, the Spice girls offer conflicting opinions. Geri dubs Lady Thatcher "the first Spice Girl"!

16 December 1996

2Become1 is released and sells more than 50,000 copies in the first week, shooting straight into the top slot.

22 December 1996

2Become1 sells more than 500,000 copies, which makes it the fastest-selling record of the year. Meanwhile, *Spice* tops the album charts.

December 1996

2Become1 is the Christmas No. 1, beating the Dunblane single to the top spot. *Spice* is the biggest selling album of 1996 and goes on to sell more than 10 million worldwide in less than seven months.

January 1997

Promo tour for the album and *Wannabe* in New York. Includes intensive radio interviews. *Wannabe* smashes into the US Billboard charts at No. 11, the highest ever entry for a British band in America. Even *I Wanna Hold Your Hand* by the Beatles only managed No. 12!

February 1997

Who Do You Think You Are video filmed for Comic Relief, featuring the hilarious Spice wannabes The Sugar Lumps. The Spice Girls' donation to Comic Relief is the biggest individual contribution. The *Mama* video is filmed featuring the girls' real mums. *Wannabe* reaches No. 1 in America and back home the Spice Girls receive five nominations for the Brit awards.

24 February 1997

It's their night at the Brit awards. They collect two gongs in total. Fans vote *Say You'll Be There* as Best Video of the Year and *Wannabe* as Best Single.

3 March 1997

Double A-side *Mama/Who Do You Think You Are* is released and becomes their fourth No. 1. The Spice Girls become the first band to have four consecutive No. 1s.

5 March 1997

Wannabe sales reach four million, making it the most successful debut single ever.

26 March 1997

At the Capital FM awards, the Spice Girls win the award for 'London's Favourite Female Group'.

28 March 1997

Top secret launch of *Girl Power!*, the official Spice Girls book, at the Virgin Megastore.

30 March 1997

The Spice Girls launch Channel 5.

March 1997

Spice, the album, achieves quadruple platinum sales across Europe...

5 April 1997

...and quadruple platinum sales of over 400,000 in Italy alone.

14 April 1997

Spice: The Official Video, Volume One released...

May 1997

The Spice Girls sign a deal with Pepsi which means that their next single comes free with Pepsi ring pulls. Pepsi record their biggest ever take-up on the promotion.
The Girls announce their upcoming movie at Cannes, where they literally stop the traffic.

29 May 1997

At the Ivor Novello awards the Girls' talents – not just their outrageous behaviour – are recognised when they win 'International Hit Of The Year' and 'Bestselling British Single in UK' for *Wannabe*. It's also Mel B's birthday.

June 1997

Their movie, *Spice World*, begins filming – but the plot stays under wraps!

July 1997

Rumours fly around that Victoria is about to leave the band. As usual, they prove to be totally untrue. Spice has now sold more than 14 million copies. Between them, *Say You'll Be There* and *2Become1* have reached No. 1 in 53 countries.

1 August 1997

It's a wrap. The filming finishes... it'll be out on Boxing Day!